THE DECADES OF TWENTIETH-CENTURY AMERICA

AMERICA IN THE 1910s

MARLEE RICHARDS

Twenty-First Century Books · Minneapolis

Twenty-First Century Books
A division of Lerner Publishing Group, Inc.
241 First Avenue North
Minneapolis, MN 55401 U.S.A.

Website address: www.lernerbooks.com

Library of Congress Cataloging-in-Publication Data

Richards, Marlee.
    America in the 1910s / by Marlee Richards.
        p.   cm. — (The decades of twentieth-century America)
    Includes bibliographical references and index.
    ISBN 978–0–8225–3437–2 (lib. bdg. : alk. paper)
    1. United States—History—1910–1919—Juvenile literature. 2. United
States—History—1910–1919—Juvenile literature. 3. Nineteen tens—
Juvenile literature. I. Title.
    E756.B77 2010
    973.91—dc22   2007042905

Manufactured in the United States of America
1 2 3 4 5 6 – VI – 15 14 13 12 11 10

CONTENTS

PRESIDENT THEODORE ROOSEVELT makes a speech in the early 1900s.

THE SPIRIT OF CHANGE

"Believe and you're halfway there," said U.S. president Theodore (Teddy) Roosevelt. Throughout his presidency, from 1901 to 1909, Roosevelt pushed lawmakers and citizens to dream and experiment. He set the tone for the national spirit of inventiveness that took hold in the United States during the first decade of the twentieth century. During this decade, Americans examined social issues, businesses expanded, and government took new directions.

The first decade of the century also saw the United States flex its muscles on the world stage for the first time. It expanded its naval power, intervened in Latin American affairs, and began work on the Panama Canal to link the Atlantic and Pacific oceans. President Roosevelt proclaimed that the United States should "carry a big stick"—or display its military power—in dealing with foreign countries.

By the end of the decade, the United States was one of the richest and most powerful nations in the world. Citizens developed the best new technology: airplanes, cars, and electric power. U.S. inventors experimented with ways to make this technology more widely available. Also in the century's first decade, manufacturers introduced new products, including paper towels, paper cups, and Hershey bars. They produced crayons and teddy bears—named after President Roosevelt—for children. Adults purchased

Brownie cameras, which let ordinary people take snapshots. Each new creation promoted expansion of U.S. business and quickened the pace of life.

Even fashion and the arts offered new promise. In previous generations, most ordinary people had sewn their own clothing at home. The wealthy had had their clothing custom-made by others and patterned their outfits after European styles. In the first decade of the twentieth century, U.S. manufacturers introduced inexpensive, ready-made clothing—so people from every economic background could buy the latest fashions. Women and girls dressed like the famous Gibson girl featured in magazine illustrations. The Gibson girl dress had a high ruffled collar, long sleeves, a long skirt, and a waist cinched by a wide belt fastened in the back.

■ SHIFTING POPULATIONS

The makeup of the U.S. population changed dramatically during the first decade of the 1900s. With increased immigration, the population soared from 76 million people at the start of the decade to 92 million in 1910. The largest groups of immigrants during this decade came from southern and central Europe and from Russia. The newcomers arrived in the United States looking for jobs and for freedoms they were frequently denied in their home countries, such as freedom of worship and freedom of speech.

The immigrants came to the United States by boat, most arriving in East Coast cities such as New York and Philadelphia. Many made their homes in these cities. Some traveled by train to midwestern cities such as Chicago, Milwaukee, and Saint Louis. A few braved the journey to rugged western towns. In most cities, immigrants tended to cluster in neighborhoods filled with others of the same ethnic background

In big cities, immigrant families often crowded into small and dirty tenement apartments. Desperate for work, they accepted dangerous and low-paying jobs. Many Americans whose ancestors had lived in the United States for generations disliked the immigrants, who spoke, dressed, and acted differently from

With increased immigration, the population soared from 76 million people at the start of the decade to 92 million in 1910.

IMMIGRANTS ARRIVE AT ELLIS ISLAND IN NEW YORK about 1900. The massive influx of immigrants to the United States from Europe changed the cultural flavor of the United States.

the majority of Americans. Most Americans were Protestant, while many immigrants were Jewish and Catholic. Distaste for the newcomers led many Americans to call for an end to or severe limits on immigration.

By 1910 the United States had forty-six states. Cities were expanding at a rapid rate. The lure of jobs, education, and lively nightlife drew young men and women to the cities from rural areas. Many of those who arrived in the cities were African Americans from the rural South. From 1900 to 1910, more than two hundred thousand blacks migrated north, mainly to cities in the Northeast and Midwest.

■ ERA OF REFORM

A host of social problems came with the nation's expansion. In big cities, immigrants clashed with native-born Americans. African Americans clashed with whites. At the federal, state, and local levels, government was riddled with corruption. Some politicians took bribes or handed out government jobs to supporters, whether or not the jobholders were qualified. Business was the scene of great inequality. At many factories, workers—some of them children—toiled for more than twelve hours a day, six days a week. Business owners earned huge profits while paying workers extremely low wages.

In the late 1800s, progressives—or reformers—had begun to call attention to these problems. They argued for higher pay and better working conditions for laborers, an end to government corruption, and other improvements in business, government, and society. Journalists uncovered some of the worst corruption and injustices during the early 1900s and exposed them in books, magazines, and newspapers. President Roosevelt nicknamed the journalists muckrakers, after a character who was only interested in raking up waste in John Bunyan's seventeenth-century book *Pilgrim's Progress*. The written publicity about wrongdoing forced government to act. Congress passed laws about food safety, labor rights, and other social concerns between 1900 and 1910.

Workers also took matters into their own hands in this decade. To protest low wages and dangerous working conditions, labor unions organized strikes. During strikes, employees refused to work. They hoped that shutting down factories would force management to meet their demands.

Police officers drive away **PICKETERS AT A STRIKE IN PHILADELPHIA, PENNSYLVANIA,** about 1910.

the first decade of the twentieth century, working women joined hands with their wealthier sisters to fight for woman suffrage, or voting rights.

Some Americans of the early 1900s believed that alcohol was the cause of many social ills. They argued that many workingmen spent their pay on drink instead of using it to feed and clothe their children. Activists pushed for a prohibition, or ban, on the manufacturing and selling of alcoholic beverages.

■ TR

Theodore Roosevelt (TR) had his own ideas for changing U.S. society, and as president, he was in a position to put these ideas into action. One of his main goals was limiting the growth and power of monopolies or trusts—giant corporations owned by small groups of people. Big and powerful, monopolies could easily drive their competitors out of business. They could set prices artificially high, buy up the competition, and control entire industries, including suppliers,

■ ACTIVISTS

Millions of women worked outside the home in the first decade of the twentieth century. Like many other laborers, many working women put in twelve- to fifteen-hour shifts under poor conditions for rock-bottom wages. In this era, women's rights were limited. Many states prohibited women from voting or owning property.

Women wanted change. They wanted good education for their children and better jobs for themselves. Most important, they wanted the right to vote. Women saw the vote as a way to gain a voice in government, which directly affected their lives and their families. In

9

LOGGERS SURVEY A CLEARED AREA in the Cascade Mountains near Seattle, Washington, about 1906. Theodore Roosevelt created parklands to protect U.S. forests from logging and other businesses.

manufacturers, and sellers. The 1890 Sherman Antitrust Act, which tried to limit the power of monopolies, had had only partial success. During his presidency, Roosevelt strengthened the act. But he could not completely rein in huge corporations. They had the support of many politicians, who relied on their campaign contributions.

Roosevelt did make headway in preserving the nation's wilderness areas. By the time he took office in 1901, logging companies, farms, and other businesses had already cut down half the nation's forests. To protect the remaining land, Roosevelt created new national parks, national monuments, and wildlife preserves and added millions of acres to existing national forests.

Toward the end of his second term in the White House, Roosevelt announced, "I have had a great time as president," but he said that two terms as president were enough (the presidency had no term limits then). He proposed his secretary of war, fellow Republican William Howard Taft, as the 1908 Republican nominee for president. Taft, Roosevelt believed, would continue his environmental conservation and business policies.

With Roosevelt's endorsement, Taft easily defeated third-time candidate William Jennings Bryan, a friend to workers and social reformers, and Eugene Debs, hero of the labor union movement. After leaving office in 1909, Roosevelt took off to hunt big game in Africa.

■ BUBBLING POT

By 1910 America's melting pot—the mix of people from different backgrounds, ethnicities, races, and religions—was boiling over. Battles over economic equality, woman suffrage, immigration, workers' rights, and drinking underscored a clash of cultures. As the melting pot bubbled, the U.S. government had to examine its laws and policies regarding individuals and businesses. Moreover, lawmakers needed to define the nation's role in world politics. Where was the United States heading in the next decade? What would new policies mean for Americans in the 1910s?

Workers around 1913 dig in the deep trench that would become THE PANAMA CANAL. The United States built the canal, which created a crucial—and shorter—trade route between the Atlantic and Pacific oceans.

CHAPTER ONE

THREE PRESIDENTS:
1910s POLITICS

William Howard Taft never matched Theodore Roosevelt's popularity as president. Taft, a former lawyer and talented administrator, rarely showed his mentor's drive and spirited nature. Roosevelt was a spunky outdoors enthusiast whose bold ideas appealed equally to factions in the wide-open West and the more settled East. Many reporters and politicians remarked that the colorless Taft governed in Roosevelt's vibrant shadow. Some joked that Taft stood for *take advice from Teddy.*

◼ DOLLAR DIPLOMACY

At first, Taft tried to follow through on Roosevelt's foreign policies. He continued to interfere with other governments in the Western Hemisphere—especially to protect U.S. economic ventures. In 1912 Taft sent marines into Nicaragua to protect U.S. lives and property after a local revolt. He also sent troops to protect the Panama Canal construction site. The U.S. government viewed the canal (which opened in 1914) as a key priority for expanding U.S. businesses.

In other foreign matters, Taft toned down Roosevelt's approach. Whereas Roosevelt had intervened overseas with the threat of guns and armies (a "big stick"), Taft used economics. He encouraged U.S. trade with foreign nations and investment in overseas businesses. Taft claimed he

13

wanted to substitute "dollars for bullets." His foreign policy became known as Dollar Diplomacy.

At home, Taft tackled a key issue that presidents before him had neglected: savings banks. Before the Taft administration, many people hesitated to put their money into banks. They knew that banks sometimes failed, losing all the money people had deposited. To encourage deposits, in 1910 Congress created the postal savings bank system. The new law allowed Americans to save money in post office banks, which paid a guaranteed 2 percent interest on deposits. With federal involvement, U.S. banks became more stable institutions.

Until Taft's presidency, state legislators appointed U.S. senators. This form of selection had flaws, since legislators sometimes chose their friends and business associates to serve as senators instead of the most qualified candidates. The system also left rank-and-file voters out of the selection process. Taft favored an amendment to the U.S. Constitution that called for popular election of U.S. senators—that is, for election by voters in each state. In 1912 Congress passed the Seventeenth Amendment. States ratified (approved) it the following year.

A Boy Scout deposits his money at a **POSTAL SAVINGS BANK** in 1913. These banks were a new option for saving money.

Born in 1857, William Howard Taft grew up in Cincinnati, Ohio. He attended Yale College (present-day Yale University) in Connecticut and then the Cincinnati Law School, graduating in 1880. In 1881 Taft entered government service as an assistant prosecuting attorney and later held several judgeships.

Taft's skill as a judge caught President William McKinley's attention. The president appointed Taft governor of the Philippines in Southeast Asia, then a U.S. colony. As governor, Taft created schools, dams, and sewers and set up the colony's judicial system.

In 1904 Taft became secretary of war in the Roosevelt administration. He also supervised Roosevelt's pet project, building the Panama Canal. Taft's success with these jobs encouraged Roosevelt to recommend him for president.

Taft never really wanted the presidency, but his ambitious wife, Helen, urged him to run. A major force behind her husband's political career, Helen joined him on his inauguration day ride to the White House, the first spouse to do so.

Taft was a likable yet stubborn man and a low-key president. He enjoyed golf and refused any interruptions during a game. He held several distinctions among presidents. He started the presidential tradition of throwing the first pitch of the professional baseball season. And at more than

WILLIAM HOWARD TAFT served as governor of the Philippines and then as U.S. secretary of war before becoming president in 1909.

300 pounds (136 kilograms) and 6 feet (1.8 meters) tall, he was the largest U.S. president. Another distinction was his frequent nodding off in public—at concerts and state dinners, on automobile rides, and in meetings with senators. Taft took so many naps while riding in his beloved automobile that Helen nicknamed him Sleeping Beauty.

After leaving the White House, Taft taught law and worked for the Wilson administration. In 1921 he became chief justice of the U.S. Supreme Court, a position he held until his retirement in February 1930. He died the next month.

15

◼ STRONG AS A BULL MOOSE

Returning home from Africa in 1910, Theodore Roosevelt found that he disliked the state of the nation under Taft. The new president backed high tariffs (taxes on imports), which protected U.S. businesses from foreign competition. Roosevelt favored lower tariffs, which would have made both imported and U.S.-made products more affordable. Taft had also failed to maintain Roosevelt's strict regulations on monopolies and other big businesses.

In addition, Taft had undermined some of Roosevelt's conservation policies. Although Taft did sign the Weeks Act, which created national forests in the eastern United States, he allowed unspoiled land in the West to be developed for water power stations. When U.S. Forest Service chief Gifford Pinchot charged that Taft's Interior Department—the department that oversaw conservation—was corrupt, Taft fired him.

Seeing his reforms diminished, Roosevelt proceeded to speak out against the new president. He attacked his former friend for incompetence. Others in the Republican Party agreed with Roosevelt. The party split into two warring factions.

Roosevelt launched a sixteen-state speaking tour to promote a more progressive agenda for the Republican Party. In speeches, he attacked Taft as stupid, calling him a "puzzlewit" and a "fathead." Uncomfortable in the spotlight, Taft allowed Roosevelt's criticisms to go largely unchallenged. Discouraged, Taft wrote to his wife, Helen, "I think I might as well give up so far as being a politician is concerned; there are so many people who don't like me."

With the 1912 election approaching, Roosevelt decided to seize the Republican presidential nomination for himself. But despite his self-doubt, Taft didn't give up on politics. At the Republican National Convention

A photographer captured **THEODORE ROOSEVELT'S FAMOUS GRIN** in 1912.

THE LATEST ARRIVAL AT THE POLITICAL ZOO

In this 1912 political cartoon, the symbols of the Democratic and Republican parties (a donkey and an elephant) stare at the new **BULL MOOSE PARTY** representative.

in Chicago, many conservative Republicans lined up behind Taft, who won the nomination on the first ballot.

Roosevelt proceeded to rage that he himself and his supporters should leave the party. "Let us find out if the Republican Party is the party of the plain people or the party of the [political] bosses and the professional radicals," he challenged them.

Roosevelt organized dissatisfied Republicans into a new Progressive Party, with himself as its presidential candidate. Roosevelt believed he could win the election. He told reporters that he felt as strong as a bull (male) moose, which led to the nickname Bull Moose Party for his new organization.

■ FOUR-WAY RACE

The Bull Moose Party had a progressive platform, with the goal of protecting working people, the poor, children, and other disadvantaged groups. The party also championed Roosevelt's program of land conservation and strict government regulation of business. In the boldest moves yet, party members supported woman suffrage and elected female delegates to their presidential convention. Roosevelt spoke of a square deal for all citizens.

The Democrats chose Woodrow Wilson, a reformist governor from New Jersey, as their presidential candidate. Like Roosevelt, Wilson considered himself a progressive. Many of his ideas about reining in big business were similar to Roosevelt's. But Wilson offered a different approach to achieving his goals. Under a platform labeled the New Freedom, Wilson called for greater personal liberty and less government control of society. He told voters, "I do not want

17

a government that will take care of me. I want a government that will make other men take their hands off so I can take care of myself."

A former professor and president of Princeton University, Wilson carried himself with great formality, unlike the spirited Theodore Roosevelt. In a speech before the campaign, Wilson declared that great leaders had to be calm and patient, two qualities that Roosevelt sometimes lacked.

A fourth party, the Socialist Party, entered the race in 1912 and nominated Eugene Debs for president. The Socialists opposed capitalism—the system of private business ownership practiced in the United States and parts of Europe. They believed that government should own or strictly regulate business so that all people could share equally in society's wealth. Strongly tied to labor unions, the Socialist Party had achieved significant victories earlier in the century. By 1912 Socialists controlled several large city governments, includ-

Socialist presidential candidate **EUGENE DEBS** speaks at a 1912 labor convention.

> **" The Socialist party is the only party which declares that the tools of labor belong to labor and that the wealth produced by the working class belongs to the working class. "**

—Eugene Debs, accepting the Socialist Party nomination for president, 1912

ing those in Milwaukee, Wisconsin; and in Toledo and Dayton, Ohio. A former union organizer, Eugene Debs had run on the Socialist ticket three times previously. His party championed workers' rights, protection of child workers, workplace safety, and access to birth control for women.

▪ A CLOSE ELECTION

As Election Day approached, Roosevelt and Wilson pulled ahead as front-runners. Both men had the ability to stir audiences. On October 14, 1912, as Roosevelt greeted voters in front of a Milwaukee hotel, a mentally disturbed man named John Schrank shot him in the chest at close range. The bullet passed through his eyeglasses case and the folded manuscript containing a lengthy campaign speech—both in his coat pocket—before lodging in his chest. The determined Roosevelt insisted on continuing to the hall where he was scheduled

to speak. Roosevelt likened himself to a colonel of a regiment with a duty to proceed under fire. "I will make this speech or die," he said.

After speaking for forty-five minutes, Roosevelt was hurried to the hospital for medical treatment. Wilson declared he would stop campaigning until his opponent healed. Two weeks later, the two were sparring again.

The four candidates drew large numbers of voters to the polls. When the votes were counted after Election Day, Debs had won the lowest share, about 7 percent of the popular vote (but double his vote count from the previous election). Taft took about 23 percent of the popular vote. Roosevelt received almost 30 percent, and Wilson took about 40 percent. Wilson also won 435 of 531 votes in the Electoral College (a system by which each state casts ballots for the candidate with the most popular votes) and became the country's twenty-eighth president.

Woodrow Wilson was born in Staunton, Virginia, in 1856. His father was a Presbyterian minister, and the Wilson family was extremely religious. The family also stressed the importance of education. Young Woodrow loved learning, especially new words.

As a young man, Wilson graduated from Princeton University in New Jersey and earned a law degree from the University of Virginia. After a short law career, he returned to school at Johns Hopkins University in Baltimore, where he received a doctoral degree in history and political science. Other scholars gave high praise to Wilson's doctoral thesis, "Congressional Government," an analysis of government and the U.S. Constitution. Wilson taught at Bryn Mawr College and Wesleyan University before taking a post at Princeton University as a professor of law and political science.

In 1902 Wilson became Princeton's president. In this position, he doubled the school's faculty, hired the first Jewish and Catholic professors (at a time when people of both religions suffered discrimination in higher education), and strengthened the science and religion programs. He also modernized the school's curriculum, teaching methods, and campus buildings. Wilson took the university from a college with limited, general offerings to a major institution that prepared students in many specific fields.

WOODROW WILSON began his career in the world of academics. He switched to politics in the 1910s.

Wilson's reputation as a reformer attracted the Democratic Party, which urged him to run for New Jersey state governor in 1911. After winning the election, Wilson fought for various government reforms. Although a stiff, bookish figure with a tendency to preach, he gained attention for his brilliant speeches, strong principles, and novel ideas. Wilson served less than two years as governor before he was nominated for president of the United States.

He served as president for two terms, guiding the nation through World War I (1914–1918). Late in his second term, he tried unsuccessfully to bring the United States into the League of Nations, an international peacekeeping body that he had designed. But he suffered a stroke late in his presidency and was unable to carry out many of his official duties. He died in 1924.

In this political cartoon from the early 1910s, **WOODROW WILSON** rides the Demo-cratic Party donkey in his Princeton cap and gown. He was known as the Schoolmas-ter in Politics.

Wilson, a shy and dignified man, seemed as surprised as anyone to win. After the votes were tallied, he joked, "It is a fine system where some remote, severe schoolmaster may become president of the United States."

At his presidential inauguration on March 4, 1913, Wilson spoke to the nation's desire for business and social reform. "We are proud of our indus-trial achievements," he said, "but we have not hitherto stopped thoughtfully enough to count the human cost. . . . The great government we loved has too often been made use of for private and selfish purposes, and those who used it had forgotten the people."

U.S. MARINES BOARD A TRANSPORT SHIP in Philadelphia, Pennsylvania, in 1913.
They are part of an invasion force sent to fight revolutionaries in Mexico.

CHAPTER TWO

OVER THERE:
U.S. FOREIGN POLICY

President Wilson had run for office on issues affecting U.S. citizens at home—issues such as tariffs, banking, and labor reform. Although well read about other nations, he had little experience on the world stage. The president understood his shortcomings when he admitted, "It would be an irony of fate if the administration had to deal chiefly with foreign affairs."

At first, Wilson's foreign policy followed the established course. He continued the Roosevelt administration's policy of interfering with governments in Latin America. He kept marines in Nicaragua, as Taft had done, and sent more troops to maintain U.S. power in Haiti, Cuba, and the Dominican Republic.

In February 1913, General Victoriano Huerta overthrew the government in Mexico, just south of the United States. Huerta ruled as a dictator—a leader with absolute power. Although some big U.S. oil companies supported Huerta, Wilson opposed the dictator and backed his political opponents. Wilson used a minor incident—the arrest of fourteen U.S. sailors in Mexico—as an excuse to invade Mexico.

The U.S. assault on Mexico failed miserably. Seventy-one U.S. soldiers were wounded, and nineteen died. Public outrage over the losses forced Wilson to pull out U.S. troops. Months later, Mexican rebels overthrew Huerta's government.

23

Fighting continued as the outlaw Francisco "Pancho" Villa then tried to grab power in Mexico. Villa attacked the new Mexican government and also raided U.S. border towns, challenging the United States to fight back. In 1916 Wilson again ordered troops into Mexico, but they never caught Villa. By then Wilson had more pressing concerns elsewhere.

■ THE GREAT WAR

On June 28, 1914, the murder of Archduke Franz Ferdinand and his wife, Sophie, sent shock waves throughout the world. Ferdinand was heir to the throne of the powerful Austro-Hungarian Empire of central Europe. The murders took place in Bosnia-Herzegovina, a region that belonged to the empire but was itching to become independent. An investigation revealed that Gavrilo Princip, member of a Serbian-based revolutionary group, had shot the archduke (Serbia borders Bosnia-Herzegovina and claimed the territory). Five days later, Austria-Hungary cracked down on revolutionary Serbs by declaring war on Serbia.

Austria-Hungary's initial declaration of war triggered a chain reaction. Russia gathered troops to defend its ally Serbia. In response, Austria-Hungary's ally Germany declared war on Russia and its treaty partner France. Other treaties brought more players into the battle. As German troops plowed through Belgium on their way to France, France's ally Great Britain declared war on Germany. The Great War, later called World War I, had begun.

In the United States, Woodrow Wilson called for both sides to end their hostilities and offered his services as peacemaker. He urged U.S. citizens to be "impartial in thought as well as in action . . . neutral in fact as well as in name."

At first Theodore Roosevelt and other U.S. leaders agreed with Wilson. They saw no need to entangle the United States with conflicts overseas. But different U.S. ethnic groups harbored

Bosnian police officers arrest Gavrilo Princip after the **ASSASSINATION OF ARCHDUKE FRANZ FERDINAND** of the Austro-Hungarian Empire in 1914.

strong feelings about their countries of origin. For instance, the nation's many Irish Americans opposed the British, who were then tightening controls over Ireland. Many other Americans, particularly those of British origin, backed the British. German Americans, numbering almost 8 million in 1914, did not want the United States to take sides against Germany, while other Americans lashed out at the Germans. As the war progressed, some committed young U.S. men joined the British army or the French Foreign Legion.

Business leaders saw the war as an opportunity to cash in. They sold arms, loaned money, and sent supplies to warring nations, mainly to France and Britain. When transporting materials to war-torn nations became too dangerous, merchants funneled goods through neutral nations—anything to keep their profits coming.

Meanwhile, some Americans protested the war in Europe. In one demonstration, on August 29, 1914, more than fifteen hundred women in black mourning clothes—carrying banners with pictures of doves to symbolize peace—paraded silently in New York City to the steady pounding of drums.

In early December 1914, automaker Henry Ford joined with peace activists to try to end the fighting in Europe. Ford chartered a cruise ship, *Oscar II*, to carry a U.S. peace delegation across the Atlantic Ocean. Their goal was to hold a conference of leaders of neutral and warring nations and to get the soldiers

Women dressed in black (a symbol of mourning) and white (a symbol of peace) march in a **PEACE PARADE** in New York City on August 29, 1914.

"back to their homes by Christmas." Ford left the ship partway through the trip due to illness. Many in the press ridiculed the women and men—mainly college students—who remained on board. Without Ford's leadership and clout, European leaders refused to meet the peace delegation.

■ BATTLE CRIES

As the war heated up, Germany and Great Britain battled at sea, fighting each other with warships, while the Germans also used submarines. According to the 1909 Declaration of London, the seas were supposed to remain open to neutral nations and warring parties were not supposed to attack nonmilitary ships at sea. Even so, both the Germans and the British stopped U.S. vessels in the Atlantic and searched them for goods that might be used in aiding the enemy. Wilson protested these actions and repeated his offer to mediate. He found no takers.

On May 7, 1915, a German submarine (called a U-boat, or undersea boat) torpedoed the British passenger liner *Lusitania*, which was sailing from New York to Liverpool, England. Although it claimed to be simply a passenger ship, the liner carried five thousand live artillery shells along with its civilian (nonmilitary) travelers. The German attack caused two explosions—the first from a torpedo shot. The second explosion has been a topic of debate. The British claimed it came from a second torpedo shot. The Germans claimed that the artillery aboard ship caused the explosion. Whatever the cause, the ship sunk in eighteen minutes, drowning 1,201 of the total 1,959 passengers and crew. The dead included 128 Americans.

An outcry raged on both sides of the Atlantic. Critics blamed one side or the other for losses of life—the British for carrying shells on a passenger ship and the Germans for sinking it. "The destruction of the *Lusitania* was a colossal sin against humanity," said Samuel Schneider of the Equal Rights League, an African American rights organization. "But the deed is done, and it behooves people of the United States to be calm . . . to stand by our President and support him in whatever course he may pursue."

Wilson felt obligated to uphold the nation's honor while reaffirming neutrality. He wrote

> ❝ **The destruction of the *Lusitania* was a colossal sin against humanity.** ❞
>
> —*Samuel Schneider, Equal Rights League member, 1914*

The World's Greatest and Foulest Crime.

LUSITANIA TORPEDOED & SUNK IN FIFTEEN MINUTES.

FOR AUCTION ANNOUNCEMENTS See Page TEN.

Daily Express 8 a.m. EDITION

BRAND'S MEAT LOZENGES.

NO. 4,706. LONDON, SATURDAY, MAY 8, 1915. ONE HALFPENNY.

1,502 LIVES LOST AND 658 SAVED.

TERRIBLE TOTAL OF MURDERERS' VICTIMS.

OFFICIAL ACCOUNT.

MANY INJURED IN HOSPITAL.

FEW FIRST-CLASS SURVIVORS.

DOES IT MEAN WAR?

THE ONE QUESTION THAT IS ASKED IN AMERICA.

OFFICIAL ATTITUDE.

STORM OF POPULAR INDIGNATION.

NOTICE!

TRAVELLERS intending to embark on the Atlantic voyage are reminded that a state of war exists between Germany and her allies and Great Britain and her allies; that the zone of war includes the waters adjacent to the British Isles; that, in accordance with formal notice given by the Imperial German Government, vessels flying the flag of Great Britain, or of any of her allies, are liable to destruction in those waters and that travellers sailing in the war zone on ships of Great Britain or her allies do so at their own risk.

IMPERIAL

The 1915 sinking of the *LUSITANIA* shocked and angered Americans.

searing letters to German leaders, demanding an apology for the act and amends for any wrongdoing. In September 1915, two more Americans died in a German assault on the British passenger ship *Arabic*. Wilson threatened to end diplomatic relations with Germany unless U-boats stopped attacking passenger ships. This time Germany agreed to warn and evacuate well-marked passenger ships before sinking them.

Many citizens and members of Wilson's administration urged him to take revenge against Germany. The killings of Americans at sea, as well as stories of brutal German attacks on Belgium, began to sway public opinion further toward Great Britain and its allies.

In addition, Wilson's advisers already saw Germany as too powerful and as a long-term threat to U.S. security.

Some U.S. leaders, including Theodore Roosevelt and army general Leonard Wood, asserted that the United States needed to act—and quickly. In August 1915, the two men had set up a voluntary military training camp in Plattsburgh, New York. Within a year, sixteen thousand men had received unofficial military training at Plattsburgh and other camps. Wilson refused to support these unauthorized troops. But he did ask Congress for a standing army—one prepared to fight—of 142,000 men and for reserves, including the newly formed U.S. Coast Guard, of 400,000.

A 1916 CAMPAIGN VAN lists reasons to vote for Woodrow Wilson for U.S. president.

■ "HE KEPT US OUT OF WAR!"

In 1916 Wilson again sought the Democratic nomination for president. On the campaign trail, he focused on his domestic accomplishments of the previous four years. These included antitrust work, banking reform, and farm support. He had also succeeded in sending Louis Brandeis, the first Jewish justice, to the U.S. Supreme Court.

At the 1916 Democratic National Convention in Saint Louis, Missouri, William Jennings Bryan applauded Wilson's domestic reforms. He particularly wanted "to join with the American people in thanking God that we have a President who does not want this nation plunged into war." The speech provoked wild cheering. After that, Wilson's supporters shouted the slogan "He kept us out of war!"

The Progressive Party held its national convention in Chicago, where it had begun four years earlier. The Progressives once again nominated Theodore Roosevelt, but he declined to run. He believed that the only way to beat Wilson was to reunite the Republican Party. The Progressives broke up after the convention, and Roosevelt supported Republican Charles Evans Hughes for president.

Wilson won the election, but neither candidate received a majority of votes. Wilson counted 49 percent compared with Hughes's 46 percent. The remaining votes went to a Socialist Party candidate and a Prohibition Party candidate. Although women still could not vote in every U.S. state, Jeannette Rankin of Montana ran for Congress in 1916 and won. She was the nation's first female congressional representative.

■ "I WANT YOU FOR THE U.S. ARMY"

Two months into Wilson's second term, Germany returned to its policy of attacking passenger ships. About the same time, the British government intercepted a message from Germany's foreign minister to its ambassador in Mexico. The note promised Mexico help in recovering land lost to the United States in exchange for aiding Germany in the war. Upon hearing the message, Americans became outraged.

By March 1917, the Germans had sunk four U.S. ships. After three years of trying to keep the United States neutral, Wilson saw no choice but to declare war. In an April 2 speech before Congress, Wilson proclaimed that "the world must be made safe for democracy."

Members of Congress greeted the speech with enthusiastic applause. They passed a resolution to enter World War I on the side of the Allies, which by then included Great Britain, France, Russia, Belgium, Japan, and several other nations. (Jeannette Rankin joined forty-nine other members of Congress in voting against entering the war.) The enemy—Germany, Austria-Hungary, and their fighting partners—was called the Central powers.

On April 2, 1917, **PRESIDENT WILSON ASKS CONGRESS TO DECLARE WAR ON GERMANY.**

President Wilson saw U.S. entry into the war as a moral quest. He told the American people that the fight pitted right against wrong. "We entered it [the war] not because our material possessions were directly threatened, but only because we saw . . . government everywhere imperiled [in danger]," he said.

"The world must be made safe for democracy."

—President Woodrow Wilson, 1917

The country braced for war on all fronts. The first order of business was building an army. Wilson quickly realized that relying on volunteers wouldn't give the nation enough soldiers, but he also knew that many Americans would be resistant to a draft—or requiring men to join the military.

To generate support for a draft and for the war as a whole, Wilson launched the Committee on Public Information. The committee enlisted film studios to make movies that appealed to viewers' patriotism. It also used posters, pamphlets, newspaper articles, and other media to build public support for the war.

With increased public approval, Congress passed the Selective Service Act in 1917. The law required every male between the ages of twenty-one and thirty to register for the draft. Draft officials then held lotteries to choose men for military service. Those selected headed to training camps.

Stirred by patriotism, many men volunteered without being drafted. Neighbors hailed them as heroes, while men who refused to sign up were branded slackers. Some women also volunteered for military service

U.S. Secretary of War Newton Baker draws the first number in the 1918 **DRAFT FOR MILITARY SERVICE.**

THE FIRST U.S. SOLDIERS TO DEPART FOR EUROPE board a train in 1917.

as nurses, ambulance drivers, and office workers. By December 1917, the nation had 516,000 "doughboys," as the soldiers were nicknamed. One of these soldiers was popular songwriter Irving Berlin, who wrote "Oh! How I Hate to Get Up in the Morning" about the hardships of army life.

As the war continued, government took control of the nation's railroad network and directed industry to produce war materials. Companies stepped up gun, airplane, and shipbuilding programs. Entire industries switched from making consumer products to manufacturing war supplies. For example, women of this era wore stiff undergarments called corsets, reinforced with steel, to shape their torsos. During the war, manufacturers stopped making steel-lined corsets and used the steel to make bullets and gunboats instead.

People from every walk of life performed war work. Normally, most businesses refused to hire African Americans or women. But with so many men at war, businesses were desperate for workers. Women and African Americans filled the jobs—at least for the war's duration. The government urged citizens to buy war bonds (a method of loaning money to the government) to "Beat Back the Hun [Germans]."

The army needed food for soldiers, so families at home cut back. The government encouraged a weekly dining schedule of "Meatless Mondays" and "Wheatless Wednesdays." Cooks substituted grains for meat. They flipped

SHEEP GRAZE ON THE WHITE HOUSE LAWN in the late 1910s, taking over the work of gardeners who had left to fight in World War I.

pancakes made with sour milk. They made frosting with maple syrup instead of butter. Some families grew their own fruits and vegetables in backyard "liberty gardens." First Lady Edith Wilson even opened the White House lawn to grazing sheep. The sheep kept the grass short, so that White House gardeners could quit their jobs and join the military. Wilson sold the sheep's wool and gave the profits to the Red Cross.

■ DISSENT CRUSHED

Along with patriotism across the United States, the war unleashed a wave of discrimination and intolerance. Feelings ran high against immigrants, especially those from Germany. Some people suspected that German Americans sided with the enemy or were even German spies. Such suspicions led a group of Texans to whip a German American pastor who preached to his congregation in German. In another incident, a Collinsville, Illinois, mob attacked a man and hanged him. The killers said that because the man hadn't enlisted in the army, he had to be an enemy spy. After the hanging, neighbors found papers in the man's home showing that the army had rejected him because of one blind eye.

The U.S. government also tried to crush dissent—that is, any political opposition to the war. The Espionage Act of 1917 stated that anyone deemed disloyal to the United States or found to be interfering with the draft or military efforts could be jailed for ten to twenty years and fined up to ten thousand dollars. The Sedition Act of 1918 punished anyone who expressed opposition to the U.S. government, flag, armed forces, or constitution. These laws (which were later repealed or modified) effectively ended guarantees of freedom of speech granted by the First Amendment to the Constitution.

Despite the penalties and pressure, a few Americans dared to speak out against the war. Some newspapers printed articles opposing the war. Many Socialists and labor leaders pointed out war's economic injustice. They noted how poor workingmen were the ones who did the fighting while industry made huge profits supplying weapons to the military. In one speech, Eugene Debs told working people, "You need to know that you are fit for something other than slavery and cannon fodder."

The government reacted quickly to such criticism. It shut down newspapers and arrested people under the Espionage and Sedition acts. Convicted under the Espionage Act, Eugene Debs was sent to prison in 1919.

ANTIWAR DEMONSTRATORS CLASH WITH POLICE in New York City in 1918.

As U.S. attorney general, MITCHELL PALMER ordered raids on radical groups.

In 1917 revolutionaries overthrew the czar (emperor) in Russia and set up a Communist government there. Communism is an outgrowth of Socialism. Under the new Communist system, the Russian government seized private property and took control of all business and the economy.

In the United States, many people worried that revolutionaries wanted to take over the U.S. government too. They were suspicious of anyone with ties to Socialism, Communism, or another radical movement. They were especially wary of immigrants involved in these movements.

In fact, small numbers of revolutionaries were active in the United States. In the spring of 1919, radicals tried to mail bombs to the homes of dozens of U.S. business leaders and public officials. The bombs were stopped at the post office and never reached their destinations. A few weeks later, eight more bombs exploded in different locations around the country. One of them blew up on the front porch of the home of Mitchell Palmer, the U.S. attorney general. The explosion killed the bomb's carrier, whom police later identified as an Italian American revolutionary.

The nation's top law enforcement officer, Palmer was convinced that a plot to overthrow the U.S. government was under way. In late 1919 and early 1920, he ordered his agents to raid the offices of revolutionary groups, political organizations, and labor unions. Palmer also shut down newspapers and magazines considered threatening to the U.S. government. Palmer's agents arrested thousands of suspected radicals and had hundreds of immigrants deported, or sent back to their home countries.

Throughout the spree, Palmer's agents never uncovered a Communist plot. Most of those arrested were innocent of any wrongdoing—but their association with radical or political organizations made them suspect. In the course of the raids, Palmer's agents routinely violated suspects' constitutional rights, carrying out searches without warrants and denying them legal representation.

After the raids, Palmer warned a nervous U.S. public that on May 1, 1920—international Labor Day—major demonstrations would erupt into a Communist revolution. When the revolt never happened, Palmer's credibility declined. In the following few years, fear of Communism in the United States died down.

■ AN END IN SIGHT

At first the United States provided too few troops across the ocean in Europe to turn the tide against Germany. The deadlock with the Central powers dragged on. Using the newest technology of the day—airplanes, machine guns, submarines, flamethrowers, and poison gas—soldiers killed one another by the thousands. They fought and died in muddy trenches, or ditches, that crisscrossed European battlefields. The number of casualties haunted President Wilson. He believed that the only hope for the human race was for the Great War to be the world's last.

The United States gradually increased its forces in Europe, shifting momentum to the Allies. The first break for the Allies came in the summer of 1918, when Allied troops stopped Germany's four-month drive into France. In September of that year, U.S. forces under General John Pershing won a critical battle at Saint-Mihiel, France. They suffered seven thousand casualties (soldiers killed or wounded) and took fifteen thousand German prisoners.

Fueled by this success, the Allies pushed the Germans back on several fronts. The British advanced with new grenades and machine guns. German soldiers—tired and wounded—began to desert their units. The German government collapsed, and Germany's new leaders made overtures for peace.

On November 11, 1918—the eleventh day of the eleventh month of the year—the German government officially signed an armistice treaty, which signaled the end of fighting. Soldiers on both sides laid down their weapons at eleven o'clock in the morning (Paris time).

ALLIED TROOPS WEAR GAS MASKS in a trench during a 1918 battle. Soldiers carried gas masks as protection against tear gas, mustard gas, or deadly chlorine gas released by enemy forces.

Around the world, citizens flooded into the streets to celebrate. "Every conceivable sort of noise-making device—dishpans, horns, revolvers, whistles, the whole category of ear-splitting paraphernalia—appeared as by magic," wrote a *Chicago Daily News* reporter. Americans celebrated with bonfires, church bells, ticker-tape parades, and mock funeral processions for Kaiser (emperor) Wilhelm II, Germany's defeated ruler. Schools and businesses closed.

The war had taken a terrible toll. Advances in tanks, airplanes, and weapons had contributed to unusually heavy military and civilian losses. The fighting claimed the lives of about 9 million soldiers from all nations combined. Of the 2 million U.S. soldiers who fought in Europe, about 116,000 died and another 203,460 returned home wounded. The monetary cost to the United States alone reached about $32 billion.

Thousands gather beneath a replica of the Statue of Liberty in Philadelphia, Pennsylvania, in **CELEBRATION OF THE END OF WORLD WAR I** in 1918.

Hospital tents shelter influenza patients in Lawrence, Massachusetts, during the 1918 FLU EPIDEMIC.

I n the fall of 1918, influenza struck in the United States and overseas. The disease spread quickly and proved deadly—especially in places where large numbers of people gathered, such as military bases.

No one knew exactly where and when the epidemic began. Suspicious Americans suggested that Germans had created the flu as a form of germ warfare. The Spanish called the epidemic the French flu. Others called it the Spanish flu—which is the name that stuck.

In the United States, nearly three in ten people caught the flu. The first sign of illness was a deep cough. The worst cases quickly turned into pneumonia. Patients sometimes died a painful death, usually within forty-eight hours of the first symptoms, although most patients recovered.

Many communities didn't have enough health-care workers, medical supplies, coffins, or grave diggers to handle the sick and the dead. In some cities, hotels and golf clubs converted to hospitals. Communities searched for ways to prevent the spread of disease. Some towns banned handshakes, public gatherings, large funerals, or funeral services lasting more than fifteen minutes. Other towns required citizens to wear gauze masks over their noses and mouths. To protect their children, mothers tried home remedies: lime chloride, sulfur fumes, goose grease, and onion syrup.

After one and a half years, the epidemic ended. By that time, it had killed about 50 million people worldwide. More than half a million people died in the United States, and more U.S. soldiers died of influenza than died of World War I battle wounds. After the epidemic, influenza lingered in popular U.S. culture. Schoolchildren even jumped rope to a rhyme: "I had a little bird / Its name was Enza / I opened the window / And in-flu-enza."

President Wilson *(center)* leaves the Palace of Versailles after a day of negotiations during the **PARIS PEACE CONFERENCE** in June 1919.

■ PEACE WITH HONOR

The war confirmed the role of the United States as a world power and President Wilson's status as a leader. Throughout the war, Wilson had envisioned a peace settlement that would not punish the losers or reward the victors but simply establish a fair and lasting peace. He had also hoped for a league of all nations to keep peace in the world.

On January 8, 1918, Wilson had gone before Congress to lay out his vision of postwar peace and ideas to prevent future wars. His list of ideas became known as the Fourteen Points. Nine of the points focused on restoring the ability of conquered European peoples to govern themselves democratically. Wilson reasoned that if power went to the people rather than to aristocrats (the moneyed elite), there would be no more war. "People may now be dominated and governed only by their own consent," he said.

Other points spoke to issues of international relations, such as trade, colonies, and disarmament. Wilson's last point introduced the League of Nations, an international body whose members would agree to mediate disputes rather than go to war.

After the armistice in early 1919, Wilson attended the Paris Peace Conference in France. Ordinary Europeans welcomed Wilson as a hero, but heads of state were less enthusiastic. They resented the United States and Wilson trying to impose conditions for peace when no fighting had occurred on U.S. soil. French premier Georges Clemenceau jabbed at the president: "Mr. Wilson bores me with his Fourteen Points; why God almighty has only ten [commandments]!"

As talks dragged on, it became obvious that Wilson's plan was in trouble. France, Great Britain, and Italy wanted to punish the Central powers. They demanded money from Germany and refused to give up land they had conquered during the war. Slicing up Europe would have turned into a free-for-all had Wilson, always the calm diplomat, not intervened.

In the end, Wilson compromised on many of the Fourteen Points. The League of Nations emerged from bargaining as Wilson envisioned. But Germany, which had not attended the peace talks, lost prewar territory and was forced to pay billions of dollars to France and Britain.

◼ AN AILING PRESIDENT

Woodrow Wilson returned home to try to convince Americans that the United States should join the League of Nations. To gather support for the league, Wilson launched a 10,000-mile (16,090-kilometer) cross-country speaking tour. Wilson already suffered from high blood pressure and terrible headaches. After 3,500 miles (5,632 km) and twelve cities, the headaches increased in intensity.

The First Lady canceled the rest of the trip, and the two returned to the White House. Four days later, Wilson suffered a stroke, which paralyzed his left side, slurred his speech, and clouded his judgment. Edith Wilson kept the public and lawmakers in the dark about the president's condition. She controlled access to her husband and limited information reaching him. She read important documents to him and communicated his responses in return.

Wilson muddled through his last year in office. Congress refused to ratify the Treaty of Versailles, as the postwar treaty was known, or to join the League of Nations, although other nations did join. In the 1920 election, Republican nominee Warren G. Harding argued that the United States should stay out of foreign alliances such as the League of Nations. In 1920 Woodrow Wilson won the 1919 Nobel Peace Prize for creating the league, but voters chose Harding as president. They were eager to put foreign affairs behind them.

39

Cars move slowly through a crowd of pedestrians on FIFTH AVENUE IN NEW YORK CITY AROUND 1910.

CHAPTER THREE

STAYING CURRENT:
1910s TECHNOLOGY

Cars began appearing on U.S. streets around the turn of the twentieth century, but these early machines were expensive and unreliable. They were open to the elements, without tops or windshields to protect passengers from bad weather. In the first years of the century, most folks stuck with horses and buggies for transportation.

But the situation was changing quickly. New startup companies entered the car business, and engineers developed sturdier, more dependable motors. Designers added windshields to block wind and rain, and headlights to pierce night and fog. Improved tires lasted longer than earlier versions and stayed on their rims over bumps and potholes. But even with these advancements, cars were still simple machines. Starting a car involved cranking the engine by hand—until Charles Kettering invented the electric self-starting motor in 1911, a major step forward for drivers.

■ THE BLACK BOMB

In 1908 Henry Ford had introduced the Model T, a sturdy, dependable, and easy-to-repair black car. The "black bomb," as it was called, was an instant success. In one year, Ford sold ten thousand cars. The next year, sales numbers doubled and demand increased. Although some people thought the Model T was ugly, it served many purposes. Drivers used the car to visit friends, run errands,

Workers assemble car bodies at a **FORD AUTOMOBILE PLANT IN DETROIT, MICHIGAN,** in 1917.

and go to work. Farmers used Model Ts to haul heavy loads of milk cans and vegetable crates. Postal workers used Model Ts to deliver mail.

In the early years, Ford's workers built each Model T one at a time, from start to finish. With this system, it took about twelve and one-half hours to build one car. Ford wanted to speed up production, reduce his production costs, and reduce car prices. He studied the work of Frederick Taylor, who wrote about mass production in his book *The Principles of Scientific Management* (1911). Ford also observed how beef processors used overhead trolleys to carry slaughtered animals from worker to worker inside processing plants.

Ford applied these ideas to his factory in Detroit, Michigan. He lined up workers along a conveyor belt, with a bare car frame at the beginning of the line. As the conveyor belt moved, it carried the car from one worker to the next. Each worker added one part, such as a fender or a wheel, to the moving car. Car after car moved down the line, from worker to worker. Finished Model Ts rolled off the end of the assembly line.

The assembly line system cut the time it took to build a car from twelve and a half hours to less than two hours. By speeding up assembly, Ford was able to

produce more cars for less money. That enabled him to lower prices. In 1908 a Model T cost $825. Ten years later, the price was $450. That year, 1918, half the cars in the United States were Fords.

■ HEAVY TRAFFIC

At the beginning of the 1910s, about half a million automobiles traveled over U.S. roads. By the end of the decade, the number had reached nine million. But cars weren't the only powered vehicles on roadways. In cities, people traveled on electric-powered streetcars connected to overhead wires. For long-distance trips, travelers took trains. Trucks carried heavy loads within and between cities. A 1918 ad for Mack Trucks bragged, "Full-powered, like a giant locomotive, the Mack truck . . . follows no prescribed track [roads] but moulds its routes according to the demands of transportation."

Alongside the new motorized traffic, some people still traveled in horse-drawn wagons and pedestrians filled city streets. The flood of cars and other traffic led to chaos in some places. Some cities posted police officers at intersections to direct traffic. Lester Wire, a police officer in Salt Lake City, Utah, devised the first-known electric traffic light in 1912. It was a wooden box with two circular openings. Two colored lights inside shined red for stop and green for go. Later in the 1910s, Detroit police officer William Potts created a four-sided traffic light, with lights for each of the four streams of traffic at an intersection. The device automatically flashed red, green, and yellow. Potts's traffic light was first installed

In 1910, when this **STERNBERG TRUCK** was built, it wasn't yet standard to have the steering wheel on the left side of a vehicle. The gear shift is outside the cab.

in 1920 on the corner of Woodward and Michigan avenues in Detroit. Fifteen more traffic lights appeared around Detroit within a year.

The quality of roads was a major drawback to car travel in the 1910s. Most early twentieth-century roads were unpaved or at best paved with bricks and cobblestones. A heavy rain could turn a dirt road into a swamp. Potholes and rutted roads wreaked havoc on cars and trucks, leading to costly and frequent repairs.

As more people bought cars, states rushed to create new roads and to pave existing ones with concrete and asphalt. The cost of paving was high, but lawmakers realized that better roads would increase commerce and boost the nation's economy. The American Association of State Highway Officials, devoted to national road improvements, formed in 1914. In 1916 Congress passed the Federal Aid Road Act. This bill created a national network of roads, with the cost of building and upkeep to be shared by the federal and state governments.

■ AIRBORNE

In 1910 air travel was in its infancy. The brothers Wilbur and Orville Wright had achieved the first successful powered airplane flight near Kitty Hawk, North Carolina, in 1903, only seven years earlier. As with automobiles, aircraft enthusiasts experimented with better engines, improved design, and more protection for pilots and passengers, but the airplanes of the 1910s were still rickety craft made of wood, metal, and canvas. Crashes were common, and only the most daring (or most foolhardy) attempted to fly.

In 1910 in Hammondsport, New York, nineteen-year-old Blanche Stuart Scott became the first woman to pilot an airplane solo. She had already gained attention five months earlier as the first woman to drive cross-country in an automobile, another risky endeavor. The following year, Theodore Roosevelt became the first president to fly in an airplane. In 1912 journalist Harriet Quimby became the first woman to fly across the English Channel, the narrow body of water that separates Great Britain and France.

HARRIET QUIMBY was the first woman to gain a pilot's license. A year later, in 1912, she made a historic flight between Great Britain and France.

WIRELESS RADIO OPERATORS train at the Marconi School of Wireless in New York City around 1912. The white paper tape at lower left contains Morse code messages tapped out by the trainees.

Military officers quickly realized the value of airplanes in wartime. During World War I, U.S. manufacturers built fighter planes for aerial combat. Flying in bare-bones planes with open cockpits, U.S fighter pilots took part in harrowing dogfights (midair combat) with enemy aviators. The United States also used airplanes for aerial reconnaissance—or information gathering. After the war, the U.S. government began using airplanes to deliver mail.

■ SOUND SYSTEMS

Radio—called wireless in the early twentieth century—was also in its infancy. In 1910 regular broadcasts of news, sports, and music were still a decade away. Instead, governments and businesses used radio to send signals long distances. The signals were written in Morse code, a system that uses short and long sounds to represent letters and numbers. One of the most famous radio messages of the 1910s came in 1912 from the passenger ship *Titanic*. After the ship hit an iceberg in the North Atlantic Ocean, the anxious radio operator sent a wireless distress signal to nearby ships.

AMERICA IN THE

An artist sketched this picture of the 1912 SINKING OF TITANIC

I n the 1910s, the only way to cross an ocean was by ship. To cross the Atlantic, wealthy Americans and Europeans took comfortable voyages on luxurious ocean liners. They slept in lush upper-deck, first-class staterooms and enjoyed fine meals, music, and dancing during the trip. Less wealthy passengers—mostly immigrants headed to the United States—slept in basic accommodations on the lower decks, with none of the fancy amenities.

Many passenger ships were grand, but none compared to the White Star Line's *Titanic*. Its expensive first-class staterooms boasted carved wooden moldings, velvet upholstery, and brass beds. First-class recreation areas included a grand ballroom, indoor gardens, a saltwater swimming pool, and a gymnasium. Not only luxurious, the giant liner was built according to the latest advancements in ship-building, with watertight compartments and a thick steel hull. The White Star line claimed that *Titanic* was unsinkable.

On April 10, 1912, the ocean liner left Southampton, England, for its much-celebrated, six-day maiden voyage to New York. It quickly gained top speed.

On the night of April 14, disaster struck. *Titanic* hit an iceberg, which ripped several holes in its hull. The ship took on water and quickly began to sink. As first-class passengers scrambled from their sleeping quarters, they soon realized the extent of the tragedy. Ship designers had equipped *Titanic* with enough lifeboats for only about half the passengers and crew. Under orders from ship officers, most male first-class passengers allowed women and children to enter the lifeboats first and remained on board to go down with the ship. The poor immigrant passengers, sleeping in the lower decks, were the last to learn that the ship was sinking. By the time they found out, most of the lifeboats were already loaded. A great many of these passengers also went down with the ship.

Three hours after hitting the iceberg, the gigantic ship vanished into the cold North Atlantic Ocean. Of the 2,228 passengers and crew, 1,517 perished in the freezing water or died in the lifeboats. A nearby British ship, *Carpathia*, managed to rescue about 700 survivors waiting in lifeboats.

News of the disaster—which took the lives of several famous Americans—shocked people on both sides of the Atlantic. Afterward, governments implemented new safety rules for passenger ships.

> **" I have in mind a plan of development which would make radio a 'household utility' in the same sense as the piano or phonograph. The idea is to bring music into the house by wireless."**

—David Sarnoff, wireless operator, circa 1916

Throughout the decade, people experimented with spoken and musical radio broadcasts. But the only people who could hear these broadcasts were hobbyists who owned special, home-assembled radio receivers. (Regular radio broadcasts began in 1920 from station KDKA in Pittsburgh.)

Telephone systems had been in operation in the United States since the late 1880s. Early home telephones allowed people to make only local calls. Long-distance calling required specialized, costly, and high-tech equipment. In 1912 U.S. inventor Lee De Forest devised an amplifier that allowed ordinary phones to make long-distance calls—all the way across the country. Three years later, the Bell Telephone Company began offering long-distance service to its customers. But the cost of long distance remained extremely high. For the most part, only big businesses used the service.

The number of U.S. households with telephones increased from about 7 million in 1910 to about 39 million in 1920. The typical desktop telephone, called a candlestick phone, was tall and thin, with a mouthpiece at the top and a removable receiver. To make a call, a person lifted the receiver off its perch and talked to an operator working at a switchboard. The caller gave the operator the name of the person he or she wished to reach. The operator then connected the two parties. Dial telephones, which enabled people to call one another directly, bypassing the operator, arrived in 1919.

CANDLESTICK TELEPHONES did not have dials. Callers had to ask an operator to make connections for them.

Telephone calling was not commonplace in the 1910s. In 1919 the typical household averaged one call every three days. Many phones were connected through party lines—one telephone line shared by two to twenty customers. This system offered no privacy for phone callers. Other people on the party line, as well as switchboard operators, could simply pick up their telephone receivers and listen to others' conversations.

■ LIGHT AND WATER

In the 1910s, many urban Americans enjoyed the benefits of electrification—the use of electric power—a phenomenon that had begun in the 1880s and expanded rapidly in the following decades. By 1910 electricity powered streetlights, streetcars, elevators, and industrial machinery in big cities.

Some urban homes were wired for electricity, but the majority remained without electric power in 1910. Families without electricity relied on old-fashioned devices for lighting, such as kerosene or gas lanterns, wood fires, and candles. These devices gave off dim light and covered walls and floors with soot.

The situation changed in the 1910s. The cost of electricity declined steadily, power companies strung more electric lines, and more homes were wired for power. By the end of the decade, almost half of all urban homes were electrified. Electric lamps and light fixtures gave householders clean, inexpensive lighting at the flip of a switch or pull of a chain. Along with electric lighting came electrical appliances, such as toasters, irons, and vacuum cleaners.

THE ELECTRIC VACUUM CLEANER was one of the most popular home appliances of the 1910s.

Frantz Premier

ELECTRIC CLEANER

MEN are quick to adopt the latest time and labor saving devices in business. The modern woman has an equal right to employ in her home Invention's most popular electric cleaner: the Frantz Premier. Over two hundred fifty thousand are in use.

Nine Pounds of Sterling Quality!
We have branches and dealers nearly everywhere. Our price is modest—time payments if desired. Booklet on request.

The Frantz Premier Co.
Cleveland, Ohio
The Premier Vacuum Cleaner Co., Ltd.
28 Adelaide St. East,
Toronto, Ont., Canada

A child reaches into **AN ICEBOX OF THE MID-1910s.** The cabinet at the top left holds a large block of ice, which an ice company replaced about once a week.

■ TO YOUR HEALTH

In the early 1900s, life expectancy increased steadily. In 1910 the typical white male could expect to live to the age of forty-nine. By 1920 that number had risen to fifty-four. For white women, life expectancy increased from about fifty-two years to fifty-eight years in the same ten-year span. Often living in poverty, African Americans had much lower levels of life expectancy in the 1910s.

The improvements for white Americans resulted in part from improved public health programs, such as city water systems and street cleaning. New laws ensured the safety of packaged foods. Refrigeration systems kept food from spoiling on trains and in warehouses, shops, and restaurants. (Home refrigerators were brand new to the market in the 1910s. Most people still used iceboxes—big cabinets with compartments for food and for a giant block of ice—to keep food cold.)

Despite these improvements, health care was limited in the 1910s. Most people were born and died at home and received little medical care in between. Scientists had developed only

Whether people had access to this new technology in the 1910s depended on where they lived. Homeowners in big cities were the first to get electric power. People in small towns and rural farmsteads had no choice but to stick with old-fashioned lanterns and candles—because power companies found it too expensive to run lines to remote rural areas.

Similarly, those who lived in big cities could hook up to municipal water and sewage pipes. They had running water at the turn of a tap and used indoor flush toilets. Rural folks generally used outhouses and hauled their water from wells.

WHOOPING COUGH.

This Notice is Posted in Compliance with Law

" Every person who shall wilfully tear down, remove or deface any notice posted in compliance with law, shall be fined not more than seven dollars."---GENERAL STATUTES OF CONNECTICUT, REVISION OF 1902, SECTION 1173.

Town Health Officer.

WHOOPING COUGH is a highly contagious disease that threatened many children in the 1910s. People with the disease had to stay home, and a health officer might post a warning like this one on the door of a sick person's house.

a few vaccines and had not yet discovered antibiotics. As a result, infectious diseases killed large numbers of people in the 1910s, especially in crowded, poor neighborhoods without good sanitation. Influenza epidemics, such as that of 1918–1919, spread quickly through cities. Other dreaded illnesses of this era were tuberculosis, pneumonia, and typhoid fever.

Children were the most vulnerable to infectious disease. During the 1910s, about one in ten babies died before their first birthdays. The leading baby killer was diphtheria, followed by measles and pertussis, or whooping cough.

Most people were born and died at home and received little medical care in between.

■ NEW ARRIVALS

The 1910s saw the introduction of a host of new consumer goods, including Oreo cookies, Bayer aspirin tablets, windshield wipers for cars, and lipstick in metal tubes. Manufacturers turned newly developed materials into products, packaging, and equipment. These materials included rayon, a fiber made from wood or cotton. It looked and felt like silk but cost much less. Bakelite, an early form of plastic, was particularly versatile. Manufacturers used it to produce everything from telephones to billiard balls to jewelry.

In earlier decades, shopkeepers had sold products from bins and barrels. They scooped the goods into plain sacks for consumers to carry home. But the 1910s saw more goods wrapped in standardized packages, printed with brand names. Hellmann's mayonnaise and Wrigley's Doublemint gum were just a few of the hundreds of brand-name products arriving on store shelves in the 1910s. To sell these products, advertisers got more creative, with elaborate ads in newspapers and magazines.

City dwellers could purchase new products in person at general stores and department stores. But those who lived far from town often found it easiest to buy goods through the mail, using mail-order catalogs to pick out products. Sears, Roebuck and Montgomery Ward (two future department store giants) dominated the mail-order business in the 1910s. Their detailed catalogs advertised the latest fashions, books, home appliances, and farm equipment. In 1919 Americans bought more than $500 million worth of goods—half of all catalog purchases—from these two companies.

Lots of new products of the 1910s were geared toward children. In 1913 toymaker Alfred Gilbert advertised a product called the Mysto Erector Structural Steel Builder. The set contained small metal beams, gears, and girders that kids could bolt together to create miniature skyscrapers, bridges, and other structures. Erector Sets, as the kits became known, quickly soared in popularity.

The next year, at the 1914 American Toy Fair, Chicago-based stonemason Charles Pajeau introduced a box of wooden spokes, spools, and rods that could be fitted together in endless variations. Fairgoers were underwhelmed by his constructions, however. So later that year, at Christmas, Pajeau hired some small people, dressed them as elves, and had them play with his "Tinker Toys" in a Chicago

A SEARS, ROEBUCK CATALOG offers the latest in fashionable men's clothing for the winter of 1914–1915.

Men's Ready-to-Wear
Clothing
Fall & Winter
1914-1915

Sears, Roebuck and Co., Chicago
Sample Book No. 89 T

John Lloyd Wright's **LINCOLN LOGS** first appeared in toy stores in 1916. They were a huge sales success, selling out in store after store.

department store window. The publicity stunt worked. Within a year, Pajeau had sold more than one million sets of Tinker Toys.

Another construction toy came from John Lloyd Wright, the son of famous architect Frank Lloyd Wright. John Wright got his inspiration by observing how his father had built the basement of the Imperial Hotel in Tokyo, Japan. The elder Wright used a series of interlocking beams to make the structure strong. In 1916 the younger Wright designed a set of child-sized, notched logs based on his father's design. Kids could use the logs to make buildings of every shape and size. These first Lincoln Logs (named for the boyhood log home of President Abraham Lincoln) became an instant success.

An astronomer took this picture of HALLEY'S COMET as it passed Earth in 1910.

I n April and May 1910, Halley's Comet—a ball of frozen gas, dust, and rock—soared past Earth for the first time in the twentieth century. Its appearance set off a minor fuss in the United States and elsewhere.

The comet's name came from British astronomer Edmond Halley, who had predicted in the seventeenth century that the comet would return to Earth every seventy-five to seventy-six years. The idea of a reappearing comet fed into people's imagination. By early 1910, with the comet due back in spring, some Americans had begun to worry. A few newspapers reported that Earth would pass through the comet's tail of poisonous gases, causing great suffering.

Even though astronomers explained that the comet posed no danger to Earth, Americans took precautions. Some sealed their doors and windows to block out the comet's gases. Others prayed. A few believed the end of the world had come. But not everyone worried. Some Americans bought telescopes or climbed to the roofs of tall buildings for a better view of the comet. Others gleefully held comet parties. From Earth the comet looked like a hazy bright object moving across the night sky. As it passed, astronomers at various observatories clicked the first-ever photos of the comet.

As it turned out, Halley's comet cleared Earth by 250,000 miles (400,000 km) in 1910, and its gases spread out so widely that they wouldn't have hurt anyone on Earth anyway. When the comet departed, the *Seattle Post-Intelligencer* newspaper summed up the nonevent this way: "The comet came, the comet went and this old earth is no worse and no better and thus far no wiser."

53

WORKERS CAP BOTTLES IN A KETCHUP FACTORY in the eastern United States around 1910.

CHAPTER FOUR

RICH AND POOR:
THE 1910s ECONOMY

The 1910s was a prosperous decade in the United States. Economic growth that had highlighted the first decade of the twentieth century continued unchecked. By 1914 the United States produced 36 percent of the world's manufactured goods. Gross national product—the total value of all goods and services produced in the nation in one year—doubled between 1910 and 1920. New industries put more people to work and earned millions of dollars for their employers.

The United States outshined its competitors on the world market, leading the world in production of cars, steel, and oil. Improved mining and processing techniques allowed the United States to generate more coal than all European nations combined. Meanwhile, U.S. farmers harvested large crops of wheat, corn, and tobacco, which they packed onto railroad cars and onto ships headed overseas.

■ HAVES AND HAVE-NOTS

This prosperity did not always trickle down to ordinary Americans. Although such businesses as Standard Oil raked in billions of dollars in profits, this money went to executives and investors and to pay for new equipment and new business ventures. The ordinary miner, steelworker, or factory worker of the 1910s saw few of the profits of his or her labor. Many working people in this decade earned less than five hundred dollars a year—not enough to adequately support a family.

55

Most factory workers were underpaid and overworked, some toiling for twelve-hour days, six or seven days a week. Factories were generally noisy, unsanitary, and unsafe. The machines that workers operated were dangerous, and on-the-job injuries were common. Workers sidelined due to illness or injury did not receive any sick pay or insurance payments.

Factory owners hired those who would work for the least money, especially immigrants and children. Bosses knew that people who were desperate for jobs were unlikely to complain about poor working conditions. In textile factories, most workers were women. In some textile factories, bosses fined workers if they made mistakes or misbehaved. Workers lost wages for "talking, laughing, or singing, for stains from machine oil on the goods, for stitches either too crooked or too large, which had to be ripped out at the risk of tearing the fabric, resulting in more fines," explained one textile worker. Often, female factory workers endured unwanted sexual advances from their male supervisors.

The exceptional employer was Henry Ford, who paid his factory workers well and limited their working hours in the 1910s. Ford reasoned that by giving workers more money to spend and more free time in which to spend it, he created more customers for his cars.

WOMEN WORK ON THE GREAT NORTHERN RAILWAY in Great Falls, Montana, in 1918. During World War I, women filled many of the positions left vacant when men volunteered as soldiers.

Burned rubble covers sewing tables in a workroom at the TRIANGLE SHIRTWAIST FACTORY after the deadly 1911 fire.

On March 25, 1911, fire broke out at the Triangle Shirtwaist Factory, a business in New York City that made women's blouses. The factory primarily employed young women and teenage girls, most of them Italian and eastern European immigrants. Two years earlier, the Triangle workers had gone on strike for safer working conditions, but their protests had yielded no concessions from their employers.

The Triangle Shirtwaist Factory operated in the top three floors of a ten-story building. When the fire started, it quickly engulfed all the fabric used to make clothing. As flames shot through the factory, some employees escaped via stairways, elevators, and the roof. On the ninth floor, however, employees found most of the exits engulfed in flames. One exit door was locked from the outside. The factory had no sprinklers and only one fire escape, which collapsed under the weight of escaping workers.

In desperation, some women jumped out of windows. Others died piled up against the locked door. The death toll reached 146 girls and women, who perished either by flames or by jumping.

At a memorial service for the slain workers, Rose Schneiderman, leader of the 1909 Triangle Shirtwaist Factory strike, summed up the situation for U.S. laborers in the 1910s: "Every year thousands of us [workers] are maimed. The life of men and women is so cheap and property is so sacred [to factory owners]! There are so many of us for one job, it matters little [to employers] if 140-odd are burned to death."

The horrific event turned public opinion to the side of U.S. workers. Reformers and some politicians cried for safer working conditions in factories. But the Triangle Shirtwaist Factory owners received little punishment after the fire. At an investigation, owners explained that the ninth-floor door had been locked to keep out union organizers and to prevent theft. At a jury trial, the owners were found not guilty of manslaughter.

57

■ WORKERS UNITE

For decades, workers had been organizing into labor unions to improve their lot. Unions tried many tactics, especially strikes and work slowdowns, to fight for higher wages, shorter workweeks, and safer working conditions. The first group to assemble U.S. laborers on a grand scale was the American Federation of Labor (AFL), formed in 1886. By 1910 this national organization of local labor unions boasted two million members. The AFL was organized according to skilled craft, with separate unions for machinists, pipe fitters, and other specialists. The organization denied membership to unskilled workers, women, and blacks, who were left to fend for themselves in fights against big business. Unlike some labor organizations, the AFL did not challenge the underlying philosophy behind U.S. business. It simply wanted to work within the system to bring about improvements for skilled workers.

Another labor union, the Industrial Workers of the World (IWW), was more radical. Formed in 1905, the IWW welcomed all workers—male and female, black and white. Unskilled workers, including many immigrants, joined its ranks. The IWW's goals went beyond simple labor reform. The group wanted to create a worker-controlled society in the United States. This radical stance alarmed many Americans, and the presence of many immigrants in the IWW further disturbed native-born Americans.

STRIKING WORKERS watch as a police officer arrests a fellow striker in Philadelphia, Pennsylvania, in 1910.

■ THE LUDLOW MASSACRE

As workers organized, employers used a host of tactics to smother union activity. They hired spies to infiltrate union meetings and learn about their plans. They created black-lists of union organizers, shared lists with other employers, and refused to hire people on the lists. To enlist public support, employers launched propaganda campaigns, declaring that unionized workers—especially those who fought for Socialism—were unpatriotic and anti-American.

Business owners often hired private guards, who attacked union organiz-ers and striking workers with threats and violence.

In 1914 a deadly labor clash oc-curred in the coal mining towns of southern Colorado. The coal compa-nies there—the largest one owned by billionaire John D. Rockefeller Jr.—completely controlled workers' lives. The companies paid miners in scrip, or company-issued currency. This money was good only in compa-ny-owned stores, so workers had no choice but to buy products there, usually at artificially high prices. Often, when miners couldn't afford the food and other items they need-ed, they bought on credit and ended up in debt to the company store. The coal companies also owned or operated everything else in mining towns, including schools, churches, and police forces. They owned the miners' houses, which were nothing more than flimsy shacks.

The southern Colorado miners—mostly immigrants from eastern and southern Europe—worked under extremely dangerous conditions. They crawled on their bellies in near darkness, breathing in choking coal dust as they unearthed coal from

A MINER DIGS A SHAFT BY HAND in an Arizona mine in the late 1910s.

the mines. Many workers died in mine cave-ins and explosions. Often owners cheated miners out of their wages. They doctored the scales that measured the amount of coal hauled out of the mines—measurements that determined the miners' pay. Although Colorado had passed several laws to protect miners on the job, state authorities generally ignored these laws and backed the coal companies in legal disputes.

Coal company bosses monitored schools, libraries, and churches to make sure miners didn't learn about unions. Nevertheless, the United Mine Workers of America (UMWA) managed to organize the miners in southern Colorado. In 1913 the miners presented a list of demands to the coal bosses. They asked for a pay increase, a shorter workday, an honest coal-weighing system, the right to spend money at noncompany stores, and other improvements. The companies rejected the requests.

With the encouragement of Mary Harris "Mother" Jones and other labor leaders, the miners decided to strike. Jones told the miners: "What would the coal in these mines and in these hills be worth unless you put your strength and your muscle in to bring them. . . . You have collected more wealth, created more wealth than they in a thousand years of the Roman republic, and yet you have not any."

As soon as the strike began, the companies evicted the striking miners from their shanties and hired private guards to monitor them. The companies also hired scabs, or replacement workers, to take the jobs of striking miners. The miners and their families erected tent camps near the coal mines and continued their protest.

MOTHER JONES traveled to Colorado to help miners form a union. She was arrested and spent a short time in prison for her work there.

"What would the coal in these mines and in these hills be worth unless you put your strength and your muscle in to bring them?"

—Mother Jones rallying Colorado coal miners, 1913

Scattered violence took place over the following months. Miners harassed and attacked scabs, and private guards harassed and attacked miners. Several people died on both sides of the fight. In October the Colorado governor sent in the state's National Guard to control the raging storm. But the violence kept building.

The exact events of April 20, 1914, are uncertain. What is known is that on that day, National Guardsmen (many of them recruited to their jobs by the coal bosses) opened fire on the miners' camp and torched the tents. When the flames cooled, miners found the burned bodies of two women and eleven children. Thirteen other people had been killed by gunfire.

The incident, which became known as the Ludlow massacre, horrified the nation. The *New York Times* reported, "There is nothing in civilized or savage warfare that is any worse than the atrocities committed by the State troops.

61

Fire destroyed the **MINERS' TENT CITY IN LUDLOW, COLORADO,** killing thirteen people and destroying the homes and possessions of many others.

JOHN D. ROCKEFELLER JR. began his business career at Standard Oil, the giant company founded by his father in 1870.

The militia is made up in large part of gunmen, desperadoes, and employees of the coal mines. . . . They . . . seem to grow in blood-thirstiness as they have opportunity to kill and maim."

The Colorado senate condemned the governor, the National Guard, and John D. Rockefeller Jr. and his hired "gunmen and thugs." Meanwhile, enraged strikers attacked the mines and the scabs still operating them. President Wilson sent federal troops to restore order.

In December 1914, the UMWA ran out of money and ended the miners' strike. John D. Rockefeller Jr., upset about negative publicity, met with union activists, including Mother Jones. He hired William King, former labor minister of Canada, to organize a "company union" for Rockefeller's Colorado mines. The union was under company control and offered only limited benefits to miners. In the end, little had really changed for the cause of workers' rights.

■ THE BIG PICTURE

President Wilson was sympathetic to workers' struggles. During his two terms, he signed several labor laws. One of them, the 1916 Keating-Owen Act, outlawed the interstate sale of goods from factories or mines that employed children under the age of fourteen, or that made children aged fourteen to sixteen work more than eight hours a day. (The Supreme Court struck down the law as unconstitutional in 1918.) Another law established an eight-hour workday for railroad employees.

	1910s	2000s (first decade)
Average U.S. worker's income	$750	$35,000

TYPICAL PRICES

	1910s	2000s
Candy bar	5¢	75¢
Bottle of soda	5¢	$1.00
Loaf of bread	7¢	$2.79
Quart of milk	11¢	$1.79
Movie ticket	20¢	$9.00
Pair of men's shoes	$3.85	$79.99
Child's bicycle	$16.00	$139.99
Vacuum cleaner	$25.00	$229.00
Two-door car	$1,200	$20,000
Three-bedroom house	$5,000	$300,000

(Prices are samples only. At any given time, prices vary by year, location, size, brand, and model.)

Wilson signed this law in 1916, narrowly averting a strike by four hundred thousand railroad employers—a move that would have crippled U.S. commerce.

But Wilson devoted more energy to the big picture—the overall strength of the U.S. economy. In 1913 he signed the Underwood Tariff Act, which lowered tariffs on foreign goods. The act encouraged foreign companies to sell products in the United States, creating competition that resulted in lower prices in U.S. stores.

Also in 1913, states ratified the Sixteenth Amendment to the U.S. Constitution (first proposed in 1909), which established the federal income tax. The first tax was a low 1 to 6 percent of income (modern Americans pay between 10 and 35 percent), but it ensured that citizens played a role in supporting the federal government.

President Wilson also worked with Congress to pass banking reform. The Federal Reserve Act of 1913 allowed the government to supervise and regulate the nation's network of banks. The act created twelve Federal Reserve Banks (FRBs) throughout the nation and called for existing local banks to deposit excess money into the closest FRB. The act also created a Federal Reserve Board to monitor the network, control the amount of money in circulation, and set interest rates on loans.

Wilson turned his attention to trying to curb big business, much as Theodore Roosevelt had done. The Clayton Antitrust Act of 1914 outlawed pricing practices, stock policies, and business contracts that limited competition and hurt small businesses. The same year, Congress established the Federal Trade Commission to regulate business, investigate and prevent unfair competition, and protect consumers.

■ FOR PROFIT

World War I provided a boon to U.S. businesses. Farmers made big profits selling grain and other crops in Europe. Manufacturers prospered with sales of weapons and other war equipment.

RIVETERS ASSEMBLE SHIP PARTS at the navy yard in Charleston, South Carolina, in 1918. Wartime jobs spurred new economic growth and prosperity in Charleston.

ARMED MINE OFFICIALS MARCH STRIKING COPPER MINERS OUT of a mining town near Bisbee, Arizona, in 1917. The removal of strikers was meant to keep the IWW labor union from unionizing miners in Arizona.

But the war hurt the cause of labor unions. Americans were united behind the war effort, and they condemned anything that interfered with wartime production—especially labor strikes. When copper miners went on strike in Bisbee, Arizona, in 1917, opponents called them disloyal to the United States and pro-German. Hired thugs rounded up about twelve hundred strikers, transported them in train cars to the New Mexico desert, and left them for dead. (An army unit rescued the miners.) Newspapers also attacked the IWW, charging that it was financed by Germany. In September 1917, U.S. Justice Department agents raided IWW offices, seized documents, and arrested more than 150 IWW leaders, effectively shutting down the organization.

Once war ended, the nation's massive economic expansion slowed. Farmers and manufacturers no longer had ready overseas markets for their products. At the same time, war veterans returned to their hometowns to find themselves with no job prospect. The nation went into an economic slump that lasted until the early 1920s.

Family and friends gather to celebrate a wedding at A FARM IN CENTRAL MINNESOTA in 1915.

CHAPTER FIVE

HOME AND COMMUNITY:
SOCIAL CHANGE IN THE 1910s

The 1910s was a time of large families in the United States. Women gave birth to about four babies each. Households often expanded to accommodate grandparents and live-in servants, depending upon family income. Fathers provided financial support, unless the family was poor. Then the entire family—men, women, and children—worked.

The average age for marrying was twenty-five for men and twenty-one for women. Divorce rates were low—about seven divorces for every one thousand marriages. The rates were low because getting divorced was not easy in this decade. One spouse had to prove just cause—such as adultery (cheating on a spouse)—to divorce the other. Women were especially hesitant to get divorced because they could end up destitute afterward. The law did not necessarily require husbands to pay alimony or give their ex-wives any property. Religious institutions also viewed divorce as against God's law. So many couples chose to stay in unhappy marriages, even in cases of abuse.

■ DOWN ON THE FARM

In the 1910s, the U.S. population was concentrated in the Midwest and the Northeast. Out west, the population was sparse. Across the country, most people lived on farms or in small towns.

People in farming communities lived much as their parents and grandparents had done in earlier eras. Rural women raised, slaughtered, and plucked their own chickens and grew and canned their own vegetables. Social events often revolved around work. For instance, families often gathered together to butcher livestock for meat. At such events, children sometimes inflated hog bladders and tossed them around like balloons.

The attractions of urban life—jobs, schools, and nightlife—lured many young people away from farms in the 1910s. When the United States entered World War I in 1917, thousands of young men left rural areas to join the army. Farm boys served alongside city boys, and they learned about one another's lives. Those who served in Europe saw terrible bloodshed but also experienced the excitement of cities such as London and Paris. A popular World War I–era song posed the question: "How 'Ya Gonna Keep 'Em Down on the Farm (after They've Seen Paree [Paris]?)" The lyrics recount a conversation between a farm mother and father. The mother announces that her sons, having finished their military service, will soon be back to a peaceful life on the farm. But the father predicts that the boys will prefer nightclubs, jazz music, and other urban attractions to farm life. Indeed, the migration to cities continued after the war. The 1920 census revealed that for the first time in U.S. history, more Americans lived in urban areas than rural ones.

U.S. SOLDIERS GO SIGHTSEEING IN LONDON after the end of World War I. Soldiers returned home with experience of a world beyond their farms and small towns.

AN ITALIAN WATCHMAKER stands at the door of his shop in New York City. Immigrants brought valuable skills to the United States from their homelands.

■ NEWCOMERS

In addition to rural migrants, immigrants also flooded big U.S. cities in the 1910s, with more than 6.3 million foreigners arriving during the decade. The immigrants came mostly from eastern and southern Europe, especially Italy, Poland, Austria-Hungary, and Russia.

With their foreign languages, customs, and clothing; their non-Protestant religious affiliations (many were Jewish or Catholic); and sometimes radical views, the immigrants upset many native-born Americans. Citizens clamored for stricter laws to reduce the flow of immigrants to the United States. Congress obliged with the 1917 Immigration Act, which required immigrants to pass literacy tests and to pay a tax upon arrival. The law further kept people with mental and physical illnesses, criminals, alcoholics, political radicals, and most Asians from entering the United States. The next year, as the nation fought in World War I, President Wilson expanded rules for deporting foreigners.

The immigrants themselves—especially young people—were eager to fit into U.S. society. Many young immigrants enrolled in English-language courses, immersed themselves in U.S. culture, and scolded parents who failed to learn English. But the immigrants did not abandon their ethnic backgrounds altogether. They generally lived in neighborhoods with people from their home countries. They performed a delicate balancing act, adopting U.S. traditions while also maintaining the music, foods, crafts, and customs of their home countries.

African American boys stand in a field of harvested sugarcane on a **LOUISIANA PLANTATION AROUND 1910.**

■ MOVING NORTH

Another group of migrants in the 1910s traveled from south to north. These were African Americans who left the rural South in search of jobs and less racial oppression in cities such as New York, Detroit, and Chicago.

Until 1900, most African Americans lived in southern cotton-growing states. The typical black family worked as sharecroppers—farming someone else's land. Most were continually in debt to their landlords and were achingly poor. They also endured brutal racial discrimination. By both law and custom, southern blacks were not allowed to attend school with whites, use the same public facilities, or eat in the same restaurants. States and cities enforced many rules—such as poll taxes and literacy tests—that kept blacks from voting. One such rule, the "grandfather clause," said that men could vote only if their grandfathers had. Since the grandfathers of all African American men in this decade had been slaves (who had no rights at all), the rule automatically prevented black men from voting.

Whites often used terror and violence to keep southern blacks from contesting this sort of discrimination. A common practice was lynching—or killing by a mob. In ugly scenes repeated hundreds of times in this decade, angry white

mobs attacked black men (and sometimes women) and hanged them. The
killers often claimed that the man
had made a sexual advance toward a
white woman—a strict taboo in this
era—although the charge was usually fabricated.

Lured by stories of high wages and
racial freedom, streams of African
Americans fled to northern cities. Between 1910 and 1920, more than five
hundred thousand African Americans
moved north. Arnold Hill of the Chicago Urban League, a civil rights group,
observed: "Every time a lynching takes
place in a community down south . . .
people from the community will arrive in Chicago inside of two weeks."

Large African American communities emerged in New York's Harlem
neighborhood; on the South Side of
Chicago; and in Indianapolis, where
the first female African American mil-
lionaire, Madam C. J. Walker, opened
a beauty products factory in 1910.
World War I added to the migration
northward, with blacks traveling by
the thousands to take wartime jobs.

■ BROKEN PROMISES

African Americans migrated to the
North with high hopes, but often
they met with racial hatred there
too. White landlords pushed blacks
to the most cramped and run-down
neighborhoods. Employers would
hire them only for low-paying jobs—
shining shoes, carrying bags, and
cleaning houses.

" Every time a lynching takes place in a community down south . . . people from the community will arrive in Chicago inside of two weeks."

—Arnold Hill, Chicago Urban League, 1919

As a black child in the mostly white town of Great Barrington, Massachusetts, William Edward Burghardt (W. E. B.) Du Bois faced racism almost from the day he was born in 1868. But little prepared him for the hatred toward African Americans that he witnessed in the U.S. South. While attending Fisk University, a school for black students in Nashville, Tennessee, he learned how southern African Americans were kept poor, uneducated, and in fear for their lives. This experience began his lifelong quest to improve the civil rights of blacks everywhere.

After graduating from Fisk, Du Bois received a PhD from Harvard University—the first African American to do so. He then took a job at the all-black Atlanta University, where he taught history and economics. He also wrote articles and books and presented passionate speeches about race relations. Many of his writings were collected in a book called *The Souls of Black Folk* (1903).

In 1909 Du Bois helped found the National Association for the Advancement of Colored People (NAACP) to combat the growing racial violence in the United States. He edited the NAACP magazine the *Crisis*, a vehicle to uncover bigotry. His fiery editorials led to magazine subscriptions exploding

W. E. B. DU BOIS led the newly formed NAACP in the 1910s.

from one thousand in 1909 to more than ten thousand in 1919. Meanwhile, the NAACP tackled problems African Americans faced in voting, job discrimination, housing, and violence. The groups witnessed a few victories, such as a 1915 Supreme Court ruling that made it illegal for states to refuse voting rights to African Americans whose grandparents had been unable to vote because they were slaves.

Du Bois quit the NAACP in 1934 and returned to teaching at Atlanta University. He again worked for the NAACP in the 1940s. He continued to write about race relations at home and abroad until his death in 1963.

President Wilson had promised to help African Americans if they supported his election in 1912. Once in office, however, Wilson ignored his promise. He and other officials did not think the federal government should interfere with state laws—even racially unjust ones. When Postmaster General Albert Burleson requested keeping black postal workers separate from white workers, Wilson supported his decision. A horrified National Association for the Advancement of Colored People, a multiethnic civil rights group, protested. Wilson responded by saying: "I honestly believe segregation [separation of the races] to be in the interest of the colored [African American] people by exempting them from friction and criticism."

In 1915 the president held the first White House movie screening. He viewed filmmaker D. W. Griffith's *Birth of a Nation*, a movie about the Civil War (1861–1865) and post–Civil War South. The movie was groundbreaking as the first feature-length film and for its use of new cinema techniques. It was based on a book titled *The Clansman* (1905), written by Thomas Dixon Jr. Both the book and the movie portrayed African Americans as either dancing buffoons or wild-eyed revolutionaries, ready to rise up against white Americans and rape white women. In the movie, saviors of the South turn out to be white-hooded and robed men of the Ku Klux Klan (KKK)— a white terror group. The movie glorified

73

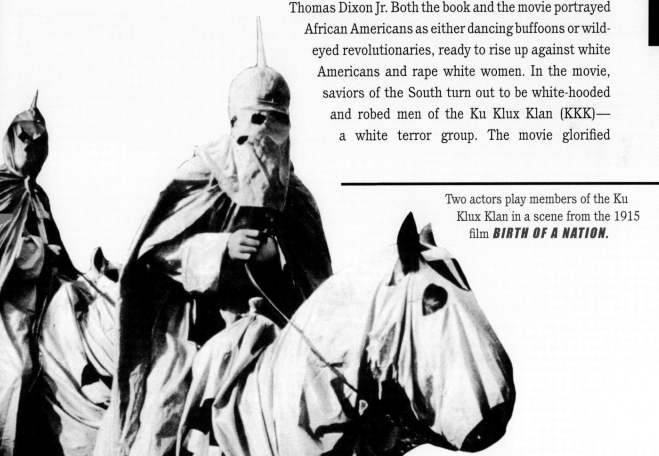

Two actors play members of the Ku Klux Klan in a scene from the 1915 film *BIRTH OF A NATION.*

the then dormant Klan and gave it new life. After watching the movie, the president announced: "It is writing history with lightning. And my only regret is that it is all so terribly true."

The president's response once again outraged the NAACP. Members tried to have the movie—or at least its final gory scenes—banned. Showings helped mobilize NAACP groups across the country, but they also boosted the Klan, whose membership shot into the millions in the late 1910s. The Klan, which once restricted its terror activities to African Americans, also began to terrorize Jews, Catholics, and immigrants in this era.

■ RACIAL BOILING POINT

During World War I, African American soldiers served in segregated units, with white officers in command. Most African American soldiers held menial jobs as orderlies, musicians, and dockworkers. However, thousands of black soldiers served in France during the war. Many of them earned military honors from the French government and were hailed overseas as heroes. When they returned home, however, they didn't get a hero's welcome. Victory parades to honor returning soldiers did not include black troops. Many African American soldiers noted with bitterness that they had fought for democracy overseas but received no justice in their own country.

At the same time, black–white tension increased among civilians. In the summer of 1917, in East Saint Louis, Illinois, whites grew angry when black workers were hired to take the place of striking aluminum workers. In July white mobs rampaged through black neighborhoods, stabbing, clubbing, shooting, and hanging African Americans and setting fire to their homes. The final death toll was forty blacks and eight whites, with more than six thousand black people driven from their homes. Similar incidents took place in Houston, Texas; Omaha, Nebraska; Chicago, Illinois; Knoxville, Tennessee; and Washington, D.C.

After the East Saint Louis riot, the NAACP organized a silent march down Fifth Avenue in New York City to protest violence against African Americans. The high-profile march finally pushed President Wilson to publicly denounce mob violence and lynching.

Members of the NAACP march down Fifth Avenue in New York City in a **1917 SILENT PARADE.** The marchers protested violence against African Americans in East Saint Louis and elsewhere.

■ LET WOMEN VOTE!

Women in the 1910s experienced different forms of discrimination. Prevailing attitudes said that men should protect women and escort them in public and that women were inferior to men. Most men believed that women belonged in the home, tending to housework and children.

State law reflected these attitudes. Many states limited women's rights to earn money, own property, and divorce, even in cases of spousal cheating and abuse. Working women experienced much sexism. For instance, one school district dictated that female teachers could not "keep company with men," "marry during the term of the contract," or "travel beyond the city limits without permission of the chairman of the board." They were to "wear at least two petticoats" and skirts no "shorter than two inches [5 centimeters] above the ankles."

For those who believed that women were inferior to men, woman suffrage—or the right to vote—was out of the question. Some opponents believed that women could never grasp politics or decide how to cast their votes. Some said that suffrage would cause women to act like men and that it would ruin families, end marriages, and even lead to Socialism.

Not surprisingly, suffragists disagreed. They countered that voting rights would give women power to reform society, business, and politics. The fight for woman suffrage had been gaining strength throughout the late nineteenth and early twentieth century. At that time, voting rights were decided on a state-by-state basis. Many states, especially in the West, had already given full or partial voting rights to women. But suffragists wanted a constitutional amendment that would ensure voting rights for women nationwide.

■ TO THE STREETS

In 1910 suffragists gathered for a suffrage parade in New York City. A few hundred members of the National American Woman Suffrage Association (NAWSA) marched up Fifth Avenue, adorned with yellow sashes that read "Votes for Women" and "By Keeping

Women out of Politics, the Soul of Our Country Is Diminished by One-Half."

Although numbers were small, the groundbreaking gathering proved so inspiring that marchers decided to repeat the event each year until women received the vote. At the march two years later, the *New York Times* counted twenty thousand marchers and five hundred thousand observers.

Opposition to woman suffrage remained fierce, however, and momentum stalled. Since the suffragists tended to support labor unions and Prohibition, many factory owners and liquor dealers opposed votes for

Flagbearers and women on horseback lead a **1913 SUFFRAGE PARADE** of twenty thousand protesters in Washington, D.C.

women. Southern states—the most conservative and traditional parts of the country—refused to even consider woman suffrage.

Alice Paul, an NAWSA member and social worker who had studied in Great Britain, saw how British women had lobbied for the vote. They had thrown notes wrapped around rocks, picketed, and held hunger strikes—anything to get attention. Paul decided to use similar attention-grabbing techniques to lobby Congress and President Wilson. She opened an office in Washington, D.C., raised money, and organized a core group of dedicated volunteers.

Paul arranged for a suffrage protest the day before President Wilson's first inauguration. On March 3, 1913, five thousand women gathered to march down Pennsylvania Avenue in Washington, D.C. Police stood guard but provided little protection as shouting mobs insulted, tripped, and grabbed the marchers. After newspapers reported how the women had been treated, an outraged nation prodded Congress to appoint a special committee to investigate. Paul's plan

ALICE PAUL joined NAWSA in 1912. She was arrested and imprisoned for her work in the cause of woman suffrage.

was working. The suffragists were gaining national attention.

Carrie Chapman Catt and other NAWSA leaders disagreed with Paul's aggressive approach. They preferred a more genteel plan that involved state-by-state political organizing, combined with polite appeals to President Wilson for a constitutional amendment.

Paul bristled at Catt's low-key plan. She split from NAWSA and formed what would come to be called the National Woman's Party. This group made headlines with more bold activities. Members demonstrated at state and county fairs, mining camps, and hospital balls. They held mass meetings and traveled door-to-door to promote woman suffrage. Paul continued the battle in Washington, D.C. Her party flooded the president and Congress with letters, telegrams, petitions, mass meetings, and car caravans from across the nation.

Beginning on January 10, 1917, the party posted round-the-clock pickets at the White House. Paul wanted to tell President Wilson that women held him accountable for their not voting.

When police arrested picketers for blocking traffic, other women quickly replaced them. The women who were arrested, including Paul, faced harsh treatment at the hands of the police. Some were beaten. Some were locked up in filthy jails and workhouses for up to six months. To protest the inhumane and unsanitary conditions, the prisoners staged a hunger strike. Police responded with force feedings.

Prisoner treatment helped win public sympathy and helped keep woman's suffrage in the spotlight. In 1918 President Wilson finally agreed to lend his support to a suffrage amendment. On September 30, he told senators: "We have made partners of the women in this war [World War I]; shall we admit them only to a partnership of suffering and . . . not to a partnership of privilege and right?"

Margaret Higgins Sanger was born in 1879 in Corning, New York. She was the sixth of eleven live children born to a mother who had gone through eighteen pregnancies. Her mother died at the age of forty, and Margaret believed that the number of pregnancies her mother had endured had contributed to her death.

Sanger became a nurse and worked with poor women in New York City. The women told Sanger that they were exhausted from working long hours. They also explained that they had more children than they could afford or take care of. Sanger concluded that extralarge families, resulting from unwanted pregnancies, contributed to poverty and illness.

The women wanted birth control information to help them prevent pregnancies. But some religious groups opposed birth control. U.S. law also forbade anyone to manufacture or distribute birth control devices or to dispense birth control information. The law said that both the information and the devices were "obscene." Anyone who distributed or possessed them could be punished with fines or jail time.

In 1912 Sanger challenged the law by writing about birth control. She wrote a series of articles, published in columns called "What Every Mother Should Know" and "What Every Girl Should Know," in the *New York Call*, a Socialist newspaper. In 1914 she launched a monthly political magazine

MARGARET SANGER fought to make birth control legal in the United States.

called the *Woman Rebel*. In 1916 she created a journal called the *Birth Control Review* and opened the first U.S. birth control clinic. Her motto was "Every child a wanted child."

Sanger's work and writings got her in trouble with the law. She was arrested and jailed several times. But she never wavered in trying to help women avoid unwanted pregnancies. She took her case to doctors across the United States and traveled worldwide lecturing about safe birth control.

Sanger kept up pressure until the American Medical Association, the main trade association of U.S. doctors, publicly recommended birth control, in 1937. Sanger continued to promote birth control and family planning until her death in 1966. The modern Planned Parenthood Federation of America, the nation's leading advocate of birth control and health care for women, traces its roots to Sanger's original birth control clinic formed in 1916.

79

In the spring of 1919, Congress approved the Nineteenth Amendment to the U.S. Constitution. For the amendment to become law, three-quarters of the states needed to ratify it. Within a year and three months, the requirements had been met. In September 1920, President Wilson signed the Nineteenth Amendment into law—just in time for women to vote for president in November.

■ ANOTHER AMENDMENT

Reformers were occupied with more than just suffrage in the 1910s. Many also joined the movement for Prohibition—a ban on the manufacture and sale of alcohol. Prohibitionists charged that alcohol led to poverty and despair. They noted that workingmen often spent their paychecks on liquor instead of caring for their wives and children.

The movement to ban alcohol in the United States had started in the nineteenth century. The leading organization was the Woman's Christian Temperance Union (WCTU), formed in 1874. By 1900 the WCTU had joined

Before her death in 1911, WCTU member **CARRY NATION** actively campaigned against drinking alcoholic beverages. Armed with a Bible and a hatchet, she marched into saloons. She prayed, sang hymns, and smashed bottles and kegs.

forces with the woman suffrage movement. The hope was that women could vote to protect families from the evils of liquor and other vices, such as smoking and gambling.

The alcohol interests were not pleased by the growing movement. Brewers, saloon keepers, and liquor dealers pressured lawmakers to oppose both woman suffrage and Prohibition. But the movement gained

steam. By 1912 nine states had outlawed the manufacture and sale of alcohol. By 1916 twenty-six states had gone "dry."

World War I gave Prohibition groups ammunition to mount a national campaign. They printed brochures showing how brewers and saloon keepers hurt soldiers by getting them drunk. The literature emphasized how manufacturing liquor also consumed raw materials—especially grain—needed for the war effort. It also stressed that people who drank were not productive workers. Prohibitionist Wayne Wheeler of the Anti-Saloon League cautioned, "Liquor is a menace to patriotism because it puts beer before country."

In the name of patriotism, Prohibitionists lobbied for a constitutional ban on alcohol. In January 1919, they got their wish when states ratified the Eighteenth Amendment. Nine months later, Congress passed the Volstead Act, which outlined how Prohibition would be enforced. The act prohibited the "manufacture, sale, or transportation of intoxicating liquors in the United States," but it didn't outlaw drinking liquor in private homes. Prohibition didn't officially begin until early 1920. In late 1919, liquor dealers ran ads encouraging Americans to stock up on booze before the law took effect.

A 1918 PRO-PROHIBITION POSTER suggests that alcohol should be banned because it makes men into unfit fathers.

THE BAR-ROOM OR THE BOY?
YOUR VOTE MAY SETTLE IT

THE BAR

"IS THAT YOU, DADDY?"

■ SCHOOLWORK

In 1910 only 13 percent of U.S. adolescents completed high school. Those who didn't complete high school often worked on the family farm or in shops or in factories. Their families couldn't afford to have them in school all day. But as child labor laws strengthened in the 1910s, fewer children worked and more attended school. By 1918 every state required children to attend school—although not all did. Thirty-one states mandated that students stay in school until the age of sixteen. As a result, the number of U.S. high school graduates tripled between 1900 and 1920.

The typical elementary school class had thirty-four students, while high school classes averaged twenty-eight. Teachers taught prescribed curriculums of reading, writing, arithmetic, and spelling. Students learned their lessons by memorization and drill—that is, by repeating what teachers told them over and over. Teachers commonly hit students to punish laziness and bad behavior.

Some educators questioned prevailing teaching methods. Philosopher John Dewey, for instance, opposed the teacher-centered classroom, in which

Harvesttime meant empty desks at a **KENTUCKY ELEMENTARY SCHOOL** in 1916. African American students were more likely than white students to miss school for work.

> **"Experience has shown that when children have a chance at physical activities which bring their natural impulses into play, going to school is a joy."**

—*John Dewey*, **Democracy and Education**, *1916*

teachers talked and students passively absorbed their words. Dewey asked teachers to become more child-centered. In his 1916 *Democracy and Education*, he urged teachers to create classroom environments in which children learned by doing rather than by having facts drilled into them.

Several school districts responded to Dewey's challenge. Gary, Indiana, for instance, introduced physical education, vocational (job) training, and home economics alongside its traditional academic curriculum. Winnetka, Illinois, worked with the University of Chicago to create classrooms in which students learned at their own pace and without grades. The Winnetka Plan also included lessons in art, literature, music, crafts, and drama. As the decade wore on, more schools expanded their programs. They added extracurricular activities such as sports teams, clubs, and bands.

Education in the 1910s was becoming more child-centered. It was also becoming more scientific. Lewis Terman, a professor of education and psychology at Stanford University in California, devised intelligence tests and published a book called *The Measurement of Intelligence* in 1916. The U.S. military hired Terman to test recruits' intelligence during World War I. In 1919 Terman received government funding to create a national intelligence test for students. Within a year, four hundred thousand public school children had taken the test.

Few minorities benefited from the new educational philosophies and advances, however. Black schoolchildren often used outdated, cast-off textbooks that white students no longer needed. School districts allocated little money to schools for African Americans. School buildings in black neighborhoods were run-down and poorly equipped, and teachers' pay was low. Many southern educators believed that black children could not grasp difficult subjects or concepts. They taught black students vocational skills, such as carpentry, and neglected studies that would prepare them for professional jobs. These policies ensured that African Americans remained in low-paying jobs and subservient to their better-educated white neighbors.

83

GIRL SCOUTS practice boating at camp around 1912.

■ BOYS AND GIRLS

Poor and working children found little time for leisure activities in the 1910s. When they did have time, they played informal games at home. Children of wealthy and middle-class families had more free time. Many of them joined organized groups, such as the Sons of Daniel Boone and the Woodcraft Indians.

The Boy Scouts movement had originated in Britain and came to the United States in 1910. According to legend, William Boyce, a wealthy Chicago publisher, had discovered the Scouts while in London. The story says that he became lost in the city one foggy night. A twelve-year-old British Scout helped him find his way. When Boyce offered the boy a coin as a reward, the boy replied that as a Scout, he could not accept tips for good deeds. The boy and his kindness so impressed Boyce that he vowed to start a similar group in the United States. His organization emphasized good citizenship through a series of character-building and outdoor activities. Within a year, the Boy Scouts of America claimed more than sixty thousand members.

The same year, Boyce founded his group for boys, Luther and Charlotte Gulick started a club for girls. They chose the name Camp Fire Girls "because campfires were the origins of the first communities and domestic life." Camp Fire Girls went national in 1912 and opened a Kansas City, Missouri, headquarters six years later. The group's Blue Bird program for young girls emphasized creative play based on family and community life.

Around the same time, Juliette Gordon Low of Savannah, Georgia, envisioned a group that would bring girls from their isolated homes into community service and outdoor activities. Low's first gathering of eighteen girls in 1912 later became the nationwide Girl Scouts of the USA.

■ MOTHERS AND FATHERS

The idea for a holiday to honor mothers went back many years in the United States—all the way to the 1870s. But the idea didn't come to life until Anna Jarvis invited friends to her Philadelphia home. She wanted to discuss ways to make her late mother's dream of a day to honor mothers come true. Jarvis enlisted the pastor at Andrews Methodist Episcopal Church in Grafton, West Virginia (Jarvis's hometown), to hold a church service in honor of mothers on May 10, 1908. Since carnations had been her mother's favorite flower, Jarvis arranged for everyone in the congregation to wear a carnation.

The idea spread to different states. People began to wear red carnations to honor living mothers and white ones to remember those who had died. Once the celebration was launched, Jarvis gave speeches and started a letter-writing campaign to make Mother's Day a national holiday. On May 9, 1914, President Wilson signed a law approving the holiday for every second Sunday in May.

Inspired by Mother's Day, Sonora Dodd wanted to create a holiday to honor her father, who had cared for his family of six boys and one girl after his wife had died. Beginning in 1909, Dodd worked with ministers in Spokane, Washington, to create the holiday. Spokane celebrated the first Father's Day on June 19, 1910. (The U.S. government didn't make Father's Day an official holiday until 1972.)

Another holiday emerged in the 1910s. World War I officially ended at eleven in the morning on the eleventh day of the eleventh month (November 11) in 1918. The end of the fighting was called an armistice. One year later, on November 11, 1919, President Wilson asked Americans to remember the armistice with two minutes of silence at eleven o'clock. The tradition he called Armistice Day continued year after year as a way for citizens to honor veterans and give thanks for peace. (In 1954 Congress changed the name of Armistice Day to Veterans Day.)

MEN READ NEWSPAPERS in the reading room of a low-cost hotel in Manhattan in 1910.

CHAPTER SIX

JOURNALISTS, POETS AND STORYTELLERS:
LITERATURE OF THE 1910s

With television many decades away and with radio in its infancy, newspapers played a vital role in communications during the 1910s. Total newspaper circulation doubled between 1900 and 1920. In most towns, readers could choose between several daily papers and several weeklies. Publishers attracted readers with crossword puzzles, comic strips, and other special features.

Magazine circulation increased in this era as well. In 1914 journalist Walter Lippmann and editor Herbert Croly founded the political and arts magazine *New Republic*, which featured writings by poet Robert Frost, historian Charles Beard, and others. Other magazines of this decade included the *Saturday Evening Post*, *Good Housekeeping*, and *Ladies' Home Journal*.

Many writers began their careers publishing stories in weekly or monthly magazines. Humorist Ring Lardner published short stories in the *Smart Set*, a leading literary magazine edited by H. L. Mencken. The *Smart Set* also introduced Americans to F. Scott Fitzgerald. His "Babes in the Wood"—the first story he ever sold—appeared in the magazine in 1919.

Written specifically for African Americans and edited by NAACP cofounder W. E. B. Du Bois, the monthly *Crisis* began publication in 1910. The first issue had sixteen pages and cost ten cents. Articles explored issues that affected

African Americans, including segregation laws and voting rights. Each year, one issue of the magazine was devoted to celebrating African American children. Although directed at parents, the children's issue also included literature for children. The popularity of this issue spurred Du Bois to create a separate children's magazine, the *Brownies' Book*, in 1920. Each issue contained fiction and nonfiction for children, including biographies of black heroes and articles about self-improvement.

■ RHYMES AND NARRATIVES

Americans of the 1910s also loved to read poetry and novels. Carl Sandburg examined gritty, industrial Chicago,

> **" Mr. Sandburg's book is extraordinarily fresh and arresting. . . . Turning the pages, the panorama of the city streets, with their daily tragedies and comedies, seems to pass before you."**

—*New York Times* review of Carl Sandburg's *Chicago Poems*, 1916

which he called City of the Big Shoulders in the poem "Chicago" (1914). Robert Frost found inspiration for his poems in his New England home. Amy Lowell described vivid images in poems such as "Lilacs" and "Patterns." T. S. Eliot launched his career with the nontraditional "The Love Song of J. Alfred Prufrock" (1917), which examines spiritual emptiness in the modern world. With her romantic and rebellious poems, New York–based Edna St. Vincent Millay helped set the stage for the raucous, youth-oriented decade to follow—the Roaring Twenties.

Novelists of the 1910s explored U.S. history and society. Willa Cather described frontier life in Nebraska in her acclaimed novels *O Pioneers!* (1913) and *My Antonia* (1918). Booth Tarkington examined families in the quickly changing, industrialized world in *The Turmoil* (1915) and *The*

Author **EDITH WHARTON** described the lives of upper-class New Yorkers in her many novels.

Novelist Willa Cather was born in Virginia in 1873. At the age of nine, she moved with her family to Nebraska. It was there, among the farms and prairies, that she found inspiration for her greatest literary works.

In 1890 Cather moved to Lincoln to attend the University of Nebraska. She intended to study medicine and become a physician, but her plans abruptly changed when a professor submitted one of her essays to a local newspaper. Upon seeing her name in print, Cather resolved to become a writer. She joined the university newspaper as an editor, began writing short stories, and wrote columns for the *Lincoln Courier*.

After graduation, in 1896, Cather moved to Pittsburgh, Pennsylvania, to work as an editor for *Home Monthly*, a woman's magazine. She continued to write short stories as well as poems. She became managing editor of *McClure's* magazine in New York in 1906. In 1911 she quit the magazine to devote herself full-time to fiction writing.

This portrait of WILLA CATHER appeared in the front of her 1915 book *The Song of the Lark*.

The 1910s saw the publication of two of Cather's greatest works—*O Pioneers!* and *My Antonia*. Both books explore the lives of immigrant farmers on the Nebraska prairie. The works are noted for their strong female characters and draw on Cather's own memories of her childhood in Nebraska.

Many people consider Cather's finest work to be *Death Comes for the Archbishop*, published in 1927. This novel is based on the real life of Archbishop John-Baptiste Lamy, who ministered to people in New Mexico Territory in the 1850s. In all, Cather wrote twelve novels in her long career, as well as many short stories. She died in 1947.

89

Magnificent Ambersons (1918), while Edith Wharton cast a critical eye on U.S. society in novels such as *Ethan Frome* (1911).

Civil rights activist James Weldon Johnson broke new ground with his novel *Autobiography of an Ex-Coloured Man* in 1912. This book, narrated by a light-skinned black man who is able to pass as white, discussed racial prejudice at the turn of the twentieth century.

On the lighter side, Zane Grey kicked off the decade with the western adventure novel *The Heritage of the Desert* (1910). He followed that with more westerns, including the best-selling *Riders of the Purple Sage* (1912). The exciting *Tarzan of the Apes* (1914) by Edgar Rice Burroughs was a hit with readers and spun off into a book series, movies, comic strips, and radio and television shows. For American girls in this decade, perhaps no book was more beloved than the magical *The Secret Garden*, written by British immigrant Frances Hodgson Burnett.

■ SPECIAL ATTRACTIONS

Comic strips became widespread in newspapers in the 1910s. Many strips mirrored the daily life of Americans. For instance, in 1912 Cliff Sterrett created *Polly and Her Pals,* which followed the antics of pretty Polly, her "Paw," "Maw," and other family members and friends. George McManus's *Bringing up Father* (begun in 1913) told the tales of an Irish immigrant worker named Jiggs. Harry Hershfield's *Abie the Agent* chronicled the activities of a lovable Jewish salesman.

The most popular comic strip of the decade was George Herriman's *Krazy Kat.* Main characters included joyful and silly Krazy Kat, a brick-throwing mouse named Ignatz, and canine police officer Bull Pupp. Another zany strip was Rube Goldberg's stories about Professor Lucifer Gorgonzola Butts. Begun in 1914, this comic strip featured the professor's outrageous mechanical devices, such as the self-operating napkin.

The first modern crossword puzzle appeared in the *New York World* in 1913. It was the creation of Arthur Wynne, an editor and puzzle enthusiast. Wynne modeled his puzzle after an older word game called Magic Squares, or Word Square. Wynne's first puzzle looked a little different from twentieth-century crosswords. It was shaped like a diamond, with boxes arranged around a blank space in the center. Crossword puzzles became an instant favorite with newspaper readers.

This comic strip from 1917 features the antics of **KRAZY KAT** and a mouse called Ignatz.

Writing and other media played an important role in the war effort—both for those who opposed the war and those who supported it. Before the war, most newspapers echoed President Wilson's disinterest in U.S. involvement in a foreign fight.

When Wilson learned that national opinion about the war split along ethnic lines, with German, Irish, British, and other Americans taking sides, he used the media to calm arguments. He directed movie theaters to project a message on-screen before films. It read, "It would be patriotic in the interest of the neutrality of the nation and the peace of mankind if the audience in this theater would refrain during the showing of pictures connected with the present war from expressing either approval or disapproval—Woodrow Wilson."

Once the United States entered the war, the president appointed Denver journalist George Creel to head a national Committee on Public Information. The committee's job was to create patriotic and prowar feelings among the public via newspapers and other media. Creel's office hired artists to create posters and writers to create press releases. The posters recruited soldiers for the military, lashed out at the German enemy, and braced the public for wartime sacrifices. One of the most enduring World War I posters was created by artist James Montgomery Flagg. The poster shows a bearded Uncle Sam—a symbol of the U.S. government—

JAMES MONTGOMERY FLAGG poses with his 1916 "I Want You for U.S. Army" poster.

pointing a finger at the viewer and saying, "I Want You for U.S. Army." Another poster pictured a sinister-looking German soldier crouching above a scene of wartime devastation. The poster asked Americans to "Beat Back the Hun" (*Hun* was a negative term for "Germans") by buying war bonds.

Very few journalists dared to speak out against the war, especially after the 1918 Sedition Act made it illegal to "utter, print, write, or publish any disloyal or abusive language" about U.S. policies. The government used this act to shut down several newspapers that questioned the war.

THE 1913 ARMORY SHOW IN NEW YORK was a showcase of traditional and
startling new techniques in art.

CHAPTER SEVEN

BOLD AND BRIGHT:
ART, ARCHITECTURE, AND FASHION

New trends in art emerged in the United States in the 1910s as artists explored the newly urbanized and industrialized world around them. A new movement began in 1908 when a group of eight artists held a gallery show in New York City. The Eight, as the artists were first called, rejected the traditional, sentimental subject matter of earlier artists—images such as idyllic natural landscapes. Instead the Eight painted realistic scenes of city life—slums, barrooms, factories, rooftops, and skyscrapers. They used thick brushstrokes to express urban energy and hardships. Detractors labeled the artists the Ashcan School (ash can is another name for a garbage can) because of the grit and grime they depicted. Rather than be insulted, the artists embraced the name and explored scenes of urban life in more detail in the 1910s.

Artists who exhibited their work at the Armory Show in New York City in 1913 took themes of urbanism and industrialization to new extremes. Many of the artists were European, but some of them—including Edward Hopper, Marsden Hartley, Stuart Davis, and Joseph Stella—were Americans. Officially called the International Exhibition of Modern Art, the show introduced groundbreaking works, such as French artist Marcel Duchamp's *Nude Descending a Staircase, No. 2*. The art on display was hard-edged, mechanical, abstract and, in some cases, baffling. The images at the Armory Show were part of a broader art movement called modernism, which threw out the rules of earlier art movements and embraced a machine-driven age.

I nvented in the mid-1800s, photography was first viewed as a craft—a mechanical process used to document people, places, and events. Along with his good friend Alfred Stieglitz, photographer Edward Steichen helped change that view. He believed that photography was an art form, and he worked to have photographers recognized as fine artists. But Steichen did not stop there. He also saw the potential of photography in information gathering and in advertising.

Steichen was born in Luxembourg (a small country in northwestern Europe) in 1879. His family moved to the United States when he was three. He grew up in Hancock, Michigan, and Milwaukee, Wisconsin. He taught himself photography at the age of fifteen.

After working for a lithography company in Milwaukee, Steichen moved to New York City. There, with fellow photographer Alfred Stieglitz, he founded a group called the Photo Secession, which was dedicated to the idea that photography was a fine art. Steichen's photographs of this era were called pictorialist. They were gauzy and softly focused, resembling paintings. Steichen and Stieglitz also opened a gallery called 291, which exhibited the work of many European artists, and they published a photography magazine called *Camera Work*.

During World War I, Edward Steichen took charge of aerial photography for the Ameri-

EDWARD STEICHEN made this photograph, "Lotus, Mount Kisco, New York," in 1915.

can Expeditionary Forces, as the U.S. Army in Europe was called during the war. Under his guidance, photographers shot pictures of battlefields and enemy installations from airplanes. The information helped military commanders make battle plans. After the war, Steichen moved on to commercial photography. His advertising and fashion photos appeared in *Vanity Fair* and *Vogue* magazines.

During World War II, Steichen oversaw all combat photography for the U.S. Navy. In 1947 he became director of photography at the Museum of Modern Art in New York. In this job, he created photography exhibits, including the acclaimed 1955 Family of Man exhibit. Steichen retired to Connecticut in 1962. He died in 1973.

■ AMERICAN ORIGINALS

In big U.S. cities, skyscrapers offered the most striking visual images. As construction methods improved and as new businesses clamored for more office space, tall buildings sprang up in Detroit, Pittsburgh, Chicago, Philadelphia, and especially New York City. In 1913 construction was completed on the Woolworth Building in New York City. At 792 feet (242 m), it was the tallest building in the world for the next seventeen years. Designed by architect Cass Gilbert, it made a striking impression with its green copper roof and ornate, Gothic-style interior. Also in 1913, then the world's largest railway station, Grand Central Terminal, opened in New York City.

Back in the heartland, architect Frank Lloyd Wright built homes and buildings for a bold new century. From his studio in Oak Park, Illinois, Wright originated the Prairie School of architecture, inspired by the vast, sweeping midwestern prairie. In designing buildings, Wright rejected the bulky, ornate, Victorian styles that were common at the turn of the twentieth century. He especially disliked the typical family homes of this era—simple boxy structures made of brick or wood.

Wright believed that buildings should fit their natural settings and that the materials to construct them should come from the surrounding environment. "I had an idea (it still seems my own) that the planes parallel to the earth in buildings belong to the ground," he explained.

Completed in New York in 1913, the **WOOLWORTH BUILDING** housed the headquarters of the Woolworth's department store company.

AMERICA IN THE

1910s

During an era when most women occupied themselves in the home, Julia Morgan challenged social standards and found great fame as an architect. Morgan was born in San Francisco, California, in 1872. She attended Oakland High School and then enrolled at the University of California–Berkeley (UC–Berkeley). At UC–Berkeley, Morgan earned a degree in engineering, an unusual accomplishment for a woman of this era.

Morgan wanted to become an architect and applied to the architectural school at the prestigious École des Beaux-Arts in Paris. The school at first refused to admit her because she was a woman but finally accepted her in 1898. She graduated in 1902—the school's first female graduate.

Morgan returned to San Francisco and took a job with architect John Galen Howard. Two years later, she opened her own architectural firm in San Francisco. She quickly proved successful, winning commissions to build homes, private clubs, churches, hotels, and campus buildings. Her significant works of the 1910s include the Los Angeles Examiner Building (1915) in Los Angeles and a Young Women's Christian Association conference facility in Pacific Grove, California (1913–1928). Morgan's

Architect JULIA MORGAN designed several of California's most striking buildings.

architectural style was eclectic, combining elements of beaux arts, arts and crafts, and other styles. She preferred to build with indigenous (native) materials, such as the redwood trees of northern California.

Morgan's most famous work is the San Simeon estate, built for newspaper magnate William Randolph Hearst. Morgan began the project in 1919 and completed it in 1939. The estate includes dozens of buildings, including the magnificent Hearst Castle.

Julia Morgan retired in 1951 and died in 1957 at the age of eighty-five. She left a legacy of more than seven hundred buildings and has been honored as one of the nation's greatest architects.

Frank Lloyd Wright built his summer home, **TALIESIN I**, in Spring Green, Wisconsin, in 1913.

Wright designed buildings that were low and wide like the prairie rather than skyscraper tall. For building materials, he used local stone, clay, and wood. He adorned the structures with repeated motifs from nature, such as images of local flowers, grasses, and leaves. When complete, his creations looked as if they had grown from their settings—whether they sat on a prairie or mountainside or in the woods. According to Wright, "Living within a house wherein everything is genuine and harmonious, a new sense of freedom gives one a new sense of life."

Frank Lloyd Wright had a long career, spanning the 1880s to the 1950s. His notable work of the 1910s includes a number of private residences in the Chicago area, as well as Taliesin I, his own summer home near Spring Green, Wisconsin.

For those who couldn't afford a custom-designed Wright home, Sears, Roebuck offered a cheaper option. Sears was already famous for selling clothing and household goods by mail. In 1908 the company began offering mail-order houses. Sears created a sixty-eight-page catalog featuring pictures and descriptions

This Sears catalog offers **MAIL-ORDER HOUSES** in six different designs.

of forty-four different affordable houses. Homes ranged from a four-room cottage for $695 to an eleven-room Queen Anne-style home for $4,115.

After a customer placed an order, Sears shipped all the building materials—precut lumber, nails, paint, varnish, and even doorbells—via railroad cars. Customers were responsible for constructing the homes on their own lots—with help from a seventy-five-page leather-bound instruction book, also provided by Sears. In addition to Sears, Montgomery Ward and other companies also sold houses by mail. The trend took off in the 1910s and continued through the 1930s.

■ BRIDGING THE FASHION GAP

Fashions of the 1910s provided a link between the formal, head-to-toe attire of the nineteenth century and more casual mid-twentieth-century dress. At the turn of the twentieth century, fashion-conscious women took their cues mainly from Britain and France. They wore wide-brimmed hats and floor-length dresses with cinched waists. Underwear consisted of stiff corsets, undershirts, drawers (long underpants), and thick petticoats. Like their mothers, girls wore layers of long, heavy skirts, with pantalets (long, ruffled drawers) underneath. Wealthy women often donned coats, hats, and bags trimmed in fur as a sign of their status.

WELL-DRESSED PEOPLE OF 1913 step out for a walk. Hats, gloves, and long skirts were standard attire for American women of the 1910s.

Slowly, through the first two decades of the twentieth century, dress designers introduced small changes. They created shirtwaists, which were high-collared blouses worn with full skirts. The hobble skirt was a slim, ankle-length skirt—sometimes tied at the bottom—that arrived in the United States from Paris in the early 1910s. The skirt was so tight around the legs that it caused the wearer to hobble—hence the name. (The skirt also caused a minor scandal by showing off the wearer's figure.) At the other extreme in terms of freedom of movement was the so-called suffragette suit, created by the American Ladies' Tailors' Association in 1910. This costume featured a divided skirt that allowed women to take long strides.

The boldest women of the 1910s wore flowing gowns and foreign-inspired dresses made of printed fabric. Clothing designers also created special outfits and accessories for various activities. Women could buy fur-trimmed ice-skating outfits and veiled hats for driving (which protected the face from dust and wind).

As new fashions arrived, women shed their stiff corsets and replaced them with less-restrictive undergarments. In 1913 New York socialite Mary Phelps Jacobs created the first brassiere, or bra (also called a bust bodice). With the help of her French maid, Jacobs fashioned the garment from two silk handkerchiefs and ribbons. Clothing manufacturers soon began making sturdier models in various styles and sizes. The first girdles, made of elastic fabric and extending from the waist to the thigh, showed up around the same time. The new undergarments gave women much more freedom of movement than corsets did and also fit discreetly beneath more revealing clothing.

Meanwhile, the fashion industry boomed. Whereas their mothers and grandmothers had probably sewed their own clothing, women of the 1910s could buy factory-made, ready-to-wear clothing from department stores or mail-order catalogs. Newspapers commonly advertised brand-name clothing such as Arrow shirts and Warner's bras. With streamlined operations, national advertising, and high-speed rail transport, clothing manufacturers could sell products nationwide. Those

"No gown can look so well without them."

—Ad for H&W Brassieres, 1919

women who still wanted to sew their own clothing could follow printed commercial patterns, with designs based on the latest fashions but for a much lower cost.

■ WARTIME FASHION

World War I brought about big changes in women's fashion. Amid the devastation of war, Paris fashion markets closed down. In the United States, citizens focused on the war effort. To save money and materials, U.S. women adopted simpler styles without jewelry, frills, or lavish trim. Many women again sewed their own clothing.

Women who took jobs in defense plants or did farmwork in place of men serving in the military needed sensible garments. Dresses with looser waistlines and raised hemlines, worn with tall, laced boots, allowed ease of movement. Even the military

AFRICAN AMERICAN WOMEN weigh cable at a factory in 1919. They wear modest but practical clothing for this dirty work.

itself influenced women's fashion. Wartime clothing featured straight lines, braiding, belts, and buckles like those seen on soldiers' uniforms.

Prior to the war, clothing had featured varied and bright colors. But in 1917 and 1918, black, white, and gray seemed like better color choices for a serious time. Before the war, most women had piled their hair on top of their heads under huge hats. But shorter hair was more practical for home-front activities. The bob—a short haircut for women—became popular in 1917. Hats also shrank in size during the war.

By the end of the decade, women's fashions looked quite different from those of 1910. Skirts and dresses showed more skin, revealing ankles, arms, and necks that had previously been covered. One clergyman grumbled, "Never in history were the modes [fashions] so abhorrently indecent as they are today."

■ THE MAN OF THE HOUSE

Men of the 1910s dressed formally. The typical businessman wore a single- or double-breasted jacket over a button-down shirt with a starch-stiff collar and cuffs. Businessmen accessorized with knotted ties and with handkerchiefs worn in their breast pockets. Most men of this decade wore brimmed hats, while boys wore caps. Trendy young men grew

Entertainer George M. Cohan *(left)* wears a **THREE-PIECE SUIT** with a tie, starched shirt, and a hat in a 1913 play.

BOYS IN SHORT PANTS AND KNEE-HIGH STOCKINGS stand with older boys and men in long pants at a glass factory in East Saint Louis, Illinois, in 1910.

mustaches, while older men often sported beards. All men kept their hair short and neatly trimmed.

Middle- and upper-class boys of the 1910s dressed much like their fathers, with jackets worn over button-down shirts. One big difference, however, concerned the length of pants. Boys of this era commonly wore knee-length pants or knickers buckled below the knee. They covered their lower legs with knee-high stockings. Graduating to long pants—at about the age of fourteen—was a sign of manhood.

Working men dressed less lavishly than professionals. They wore inexpensive jackets, trousers, and button-down shirts—sometimes made at home. Farmers wore sturdy bib overalls and other rugged clothing. Many service workers, such as waiters, train porters, and delivery men, wore job-specific uniforms.

■ PAINTED LADIES

In the early 1900s, wearing makeup was taboo. It sent a signal that a woman had loose morals—or worst of all was a prostitute. Actresses wore makeup, and they too had shady reputations.

ELIZABETH ARDEN introduced eye makeup and cosmetic makeovers to U.S. women during the 1910s.

But attitudes began changing in the 1910s. Actresses who appeared in motion pictures—a brand-new industry in this decade—became celebrities and trendsetters. Ordinary women wanted to copy movie actresses and advertising models. They wanted to enhance and show off their looks.

Women also wanted to use makeup, and manufacturers were quick to oblige them. One of several Americans to jump into the makeup business in the 1910s was New York chemist T. L. Williams. In 1915 he watched his sister Mabel apply petroleum jelly and coal dust to her eyelashes to darken them. Mabel wanted lush dark lashes like those of popular screen actresses. In his laboratory, Williams cooked up his own lash darkener, or mascara, and named his company Maybelline, after his sister.

Russian immigrant Max Factor began his cosmetics business producing face paint and powder for stage actors. In the 1910s, he made makeup specifically for movie actors and then for ordinary women at home. Elizabeth Arden (originally named Florence Nightingale Graham) opened a beauty salon on Fifth Avenue in New York City in 1910 and soon had launched her own line of cosmetics and skin-care products. In 1915 manufacturer Maurice Levy developed lipstick in a metal tube. By the end of the decade, makeup on women—especially young women—was no longer considered scandalous.

FOUR DANCERS FROM THE ZIEGFELD FOLLIES pose in lacy dresses and elaborate hats in an advertisement for a 1915 show.

CHAPTER EIGHT

SHOW BIZ:
LIVE THEATER AND MUSIC

Vaudeville, begun in the 1890s, remained a popular form of live entertainment in the 1910s. Vaudeville houses in cities across the United States offered several shows a day, with acts by singers, dancers, comics, magicians, and even performing animals. Future stars Jack Benny, George Burns, and Mae West all launched their show-business careers in vaudeville in the 1910s. Performers often traveled the "vaudeville circuit," taking their acts from city to city.

Beginning in 1907, New York show business promoter Florenz (Flo) Ziegfeld brought the mix of song, dance, and comedy to new heights. He produced spectacular variety shows, highlighted by his Ziegfeld Girls—a chorus line of shapely women dressed in big headdresses and scanty costumes. The women strutted across the stage to songs such as "A Pretty Girl Is Like a Melody" (1918), penned by Irving Berlin. The Ziegfeld Follies, as the shows were called, launched the careers of many show business greats. They included comic and later film star W. C. Fields and cowboy humorist Will Rogers, as well as Eddie Cantor, Bert Williams, and Fanny Brice—who were both singers and comedians.

Ziegfeld's theater was one of many on Broadway in New York City. Called the Great White Way because the theaters lit white lightbulbs in their marquees, Broadway was the center of live theater in the United States. Theatergoers flocked there to see musical comedies, musical reviews, and dramatic plays.

In the 1910s, it was uncommon to see African Americans onstage or in the movies. A few film studios made "race movies" for African American audiences, and theaters in African American neighborhoods put on all-black shows. But mainstream white audiences rarely, if ever, saw a black actor or performer. In many early films, such as *Birth of a Nation*, white actors played black characters by darkening their faces with burned cork or greasepaint. These "blackface" portrayals usually played up the most insulting stereotypes about African Americans.

The black performer Bert Williams entered show business during this very racist time. Williams was born in Antigua, an island in the West Indies, but grew up in New York and California. After high school, he started singing in minstrel shows. These live performances usually featured white performers with their faces blackened to look like African Americans. Even though Williams was black, he darkened his face too.

Williams soon developed a popular act combining singing, dancing, and comedy. In 1893 he teamed up with George Walker, another African American. They developed a popular routine, with Walker playing a slick-talking schemer and Williams playing a fool. Williams and Walker played the vaudeville circuit for the next seventeen years. They also recorded songs for the Victor and Columbia record companies. One song, "Nobody," became Williams's theme song.

BERT WILLIAMS wears blackface makeup in a Ziegfeld Follies photograph from the 1910s.

After George Walker died in 1910, Williams launched a solo career. Flo Ziegfeld signed him as a featured performer for his Follies, a move that shocked some white performers and audience members. Never before had a black man starred in a major Broadway revue. When some white performers said they'd quit if Williams appeared with them, Ziegfeld called their bluff and threatened to fire them.

Williams stayed with the Follies for the next ten years, delighting audiences and becoming the show's highest-paid male performer. During that time, Williams recorded several hit songs, including "Play That Barber Shop Chord" (1910) and "It's Nobody's Business but My Own" (1919). Williams died in 1922, aged only forty-six. He is remembered for his brilliant humor as well as for breaking the color barrier in show business.

> **" Have proceeded to California. Want authority to rent barn in a place called Hollywood for $75 a month."**

—Cecil B. DeMille, director, in a telegram to studio boss Jesse Lasky, 1913

■ MOVING PICTURES

Movies were still a new invention in the 1910s, but they attracted big audiences. All the films of this era were silent, because the technology for sound films had not yet been invented. And at the beginning of the decade, all the films were short—usually ten to twelve minutes. The first feature-length film (running about two hours) was the racially inflammatory *Birth of a Nation*, released in 1915.

Most early movies were sappy melodramas, slapstick comedies, or action-packed westerns. Since the films had no sounds or spoken words, filmmakers inserted titles between scenes, with printed dialogue or descriptions of the action. To enhance the mood of shows, theater owners often hired piano players to accompany the on-screen action with lively or somber melodies.

Thomas Edison, who had invented early motion picture equipment, controlled much of the movie industry with his Motion Picture Patents Company. He produced many movies, including the first version of *Frankenstein* (1910). To compete with Edison, independent producers set up studios in New York, New Jersey and, finally, Hollywood, California. Competition for talent was fierce, and film studios often raided one another's acting companies to hire away dashing leading men or flirty young women.

Like most theaters of the 1910s, this **SAN FRANCISCO CINEMA** showed back-to-back films. Viewers watched several fifteen- to twenty-minute movies at a time.

1910s

AMERICA IN THE

Mary Pickford—called America's Sweetheart—was Hollywood's first movie star. Born in Toronto, Canada, in 1892, Pickford started acting onstage at the age of five and acted in her first movie at the age of seventeen. Unlike many movie actors of this era, who performed as though they were acting for live audiences in a theater, Pickford played to the camera close-up. In this era of silent film, her gestures and facial expressions conveyed strong messages.

Audiences loved Pickford, and studios fought for her. She moved from one film studio to another, each time negotiating better contracts. By the age of twenty-one, Pickford earned for just one film what most other actors earned in a year. Pickford played every sort of female role—both strong women and weak ones. But she is most remembered for playing girls in films such as *The Poor Little Rich Girl* (1917) and *Rebecca of Sunnybrook Farm* (1917).

During World War I, Pickford joined fellow actors Charlie Chaplin and Douglas Fairbanks (whom she later married) in

MARY PICKFORD stars as a lonely child in the 1917 silent film *The Poor Little Rich Girl.*

encouraging Americans to buy war bonds. In 1919 the three powerhouse actors, with director D. W. Griffith, formed the Los Angeles–based movie studio United Artists.

In the 1920s, Pickford helped lead United Artists and acted in movies, although not as many as she had made in the 1910s. She won an Academy Award for her performance in *Coquette* (1929)—her first talkie, or sound film. Pickford acted in her last film in 1933. She remained active in the movie industry until her death in 1979.

THE KEYSTONE KOPS, a group of incompetent police officers, begin another misadventure in the 1913 film *The Gangsters*. Over time, the Kops moved out of the starring roles and instead supported popular actors such as Roscoe "Fatty" Arbuckle *(right)* in feature films.

■ BIG BUSINESS

By the early teens, it was clear that movies had won a permanent place in U.S. culture. Studios branched out into science fiction, horror, and other genres. A film version of Jules Verne's 1890 novel *Twenty Thousand Leagues under the Sea* made film history in 1916 with underwater footage shot in the Bahamas. Edgar Rice Burroughs's novel *Tarzan of the Apes* became a film two years later.

The Keystone Film Company, founded by Mack Sennett, produced hundreds of film comedies in the 1910s. Many of these movies featured the antics of the hapless Keystone Kops. Instead of solving people's problems, these goofy police officers usually made them worse.

Along with movies of the 1910s came movie stars. The female stars of this decade included the mysterious and dark-eyed Theda Bara, who usually played the vamp, a heavily made-up, seductive female. ("Kiss me, my fool," she demanded of an on-screen lover in *A Fool There Was* in 1915.) Sisters Dorothy and Lillian Gish played more wholesome heroines, as did Mary Pickford, who was nicknamed America's Sweetheart.

By far the biggest male star of the 1910s was British-born Charlie Chaplin, who acted in films that he also wrote and produced. In movies such as *The Tramp* (1915) and *The Floorwalker* (1916), he usually played a shuffling, shabbily dressed hobo. No matter what hardships the little tramp faced, he always bounced back in the end.

By the late 1910s, movie studios had found a permanent home in Hollywood. There they created everything from sweet romantic comedies to big-budget

THEDA BARA wears an elaborate dress finished with a train of peacock feathers in the 1917 film *Cleopatra*.

CHARLIE CHAPLIN *(center)* plays an inept soldier sent to war in France in the 1918 film *Shoulder Arms*.

epics with extras numbering in the thousands. Even directors, including D. W. Griffith and Cecil B. DeMille, had become famous.

Across the nation, movie attendance soared as Americans of all ages crowded into neighborhood theaters. Before the main attraction, moviegoers watched one or two short films, cartoons, and newsreels (short news films), and sometimes even live music and other performances—all for about twenty cents.

Children dance to music played on a VICTROLA at a school in rural Wisconsin in 1919.

CHAPTER NINE

UP-TEMPO:
MUSIC OF THE 1910s

Americans of the 1910s loved music—both making it and listening to it. Families and friends often gathered around a piano for sing-alongs in the family parlor. The piano player and sometimes other musicians read the notes from sheet music.

People couldn't learn songs from the radio, since this technology was in its experimental stages in the 1910s, but they did hear music at vaudeville and Broadway shows. They also learned from phonograph recordings. After a song debuted at a show or on a record, people often rushed out to buy the sheet music, and big sheet music sales were a sign that a song was a hit. The area around Twenty-eighth Street in New York City—nicknamed Tin Pan Alley—was the center of the sheet music publishing business in this era.

Phonograph recordings were a fairly new invention in the 1910s—only a little more than a decade old. The recordings were made on shellac disks called, appropriately enough, records. To play a record, one needed a phonograph machine, which reproduced the sounds as the disk spun around.

The Victrola, made by the Victor Talking Machine Company, was a popular 1910s record player. The machine had a base for spinning records and a big horn that served as a speaker. Early Victrolas had to be wound up. The user

OPERA SINGER GERALDINE FARRAR poses with a Victrola in a 1915 ad for her new recording of the opera *Carmen*. Farrar also starred in a silent film version of *Carmen*. She was one of the first classical musicians to promote herself onstage, on-screen, and on records at the same time.

turned a crank, which started the machine spinning. In 1913 Victor introduced a phonograph with an electric motor, which eliminated the need for hand cranking.

Americans listened to opera and classical music on records. But catchy songs such as "Waiting for the Robert E. Lee," sung by Al Jolson, proved more popular. As more and more people bought record players, listening to music replaced the old-fashioned sing-along. Sales of sheet music dropped.

Music played a big role in the labor movement in the early twentieth century. At union meetings and during strikes, workers often sang to bolster one another's spirits and to create group solidarity. Joe Hill, a Swedish immigrant, wrote many of the songs the workers sang.

Hill was born in 1879 in Sweden. His real name was Joel Hagglund. He changed that to Joe Hill when he moved to the United States in 1902.

Hill traveled the nation, hitching rides on freight cars and taking whatever jobs he could find. He worked in coal mines and on the docks in California. In 1910 he joined the Socialist labor group Industrial Workers of the World. He became an IWW leader, making speeches and helping to organize other workers.

Hill began writing songs and poems to unite workers behind the union cause. The songs mainly consisted of new lyrics written to familiar tunes. One song, "The Preacher and the Slave," attacked preachers who promised working people "pie in the sky"—that is, rewards for their hard work in heaven after they'd endured a living hell as laborers in dangerous factories and mines. Hill's other famous songs included "Rebel Girl" and "There Is Power in a Union."

Joe Hill became a martyr to the union movement after he was arrested for murdering two men in Salt Lake City, Utah, in 1914.

This portrait of JOE HILL appears on a postcard labeled "Joe Hill's Last Will—Don't mourn but organize."

All the evidence pointed to Hill's innocence, but the authorities despised him as a Socialist and a labor leader. After a trial that many called unfair, a jury sentenced Hill to death. An appeal to the Utah Supreme Court was unsuccessful. Even President Wilson tried to step in to save Hill's life, but the execution went forward. Hill died by firing squad on November 19, 1915. In a letter written to a fellow labor leader right before his death, Hill advised, "Don't waste time mourning [for me]. Organize."

In the following decades, Hill became a hero to labor and left-wing causes. Other musicians wrote poems and songs in his honor. The most famous was "I Dreamed I Saw Joe Hill Last Night," written in the 1930s.

AMERICA IN THE

encouraged young men to join the army
during World War I.

■ WORDS AND MELODIES

Some of the most popular songs of
the 1910s were George M. Cohan's
"Over There," a patriotic World
War I song, and George Gershwin's "Swanee," which praised
life on the Suwannee River in
the U.S. South. Both Cohan and
Gershwin churned out beloved
popular songs for the next two
decades.

Irving Berlin was another
top songwriter of the 1910s.
Berlin could play piano by ear
but in only one key. This limi-
tation made little difference
in his ability to create some
of the most memorable tunes
of the day. His "Alexander's
Ragtime Band" (1911) sold one million copies of sheet music
within months of its debut in a vaudeville show.

Jazz music had deep roots in the African American community in the
southern United States—particularly in New Orleans, Louisiana. In the
early twentieth century, jazz came north with the African American migration. Jazz clubs opened in Chicago, New York, and other northern cities.
Musicians such as King Oliver helped spread the music not just in African
American neighborhoods but also to white players and audiences.

Blues music, which had its origins in African American work songs, also
came north with the Great Migration. The lead blues player in the 1910s was

JOE "KING" OLIVER *(left)* AND W. C. HANDY *(right)* were two of the most influential American composers of the 1910s. Oliver played with jazz bands around the United States and later formed his own band. Handy is often called the father of the blues.

W. C. Handy, who popularized the genre with his "St. Louis Blues" and "Beale Street Blues."

◼ "OVER THERE"

When World War I began in Europe, the United States turned its thoughts to war. Music with a steady beat and songs with stirring lyrics aroused people's patriotism. Even though the United States hadn't yet entered the fight, songwriters began penning war songs. "Sister Susie's Sewing Shirts for Soldiers" and "Good-bye Little Girl Good-bye" prepared families for the possibility of loved ones going overseas to fight. But antiwar songs arrived too. "When Angels Weep" (1914) encouraged listeners to pray for peace, while "I Didn't Raise My Boy to Be a Soldier" (1915) looked at the tragedy of warfare from a mother's point of view.

Much social life in the 1910s centered on dancing. Couples flocked to ballrooms to dance the fox-trot (popularized by Harry Fox in his Ziegfeld Follies routine), as well as the turkey trot, the grizzly bear, and the bunny hug. The exotic tango, a Latin American import, also arrived in ballrooms during this period.

The husband-and-wife dance team of Vernon and Irene Castle did much to heighten the dance craze of the 1910s. British-born comedian Vernon Castle met dancer Irene Foote in 1910 in New Rochelle, New York, where she was born. The two married a year later. They formed a dance partnership as well.

After gaining fame in Paris in 1912, the couple returned to the United States. They opened a dancing school and performed at nightclubs and in musical shows. Their greatest fame came in Irving Berlin's Broadway musical *Watch Your Step*.

The Castles introduced several new dances, most famously the Castle walk. They also set off fashion trends. Men imitated Vernon's smooth moves on the dance floor. Women styled themselves after Irene, who wore bobbed hair, headbands,

IRENE AND VERNON CASTLE perform in the late 1910s.

and flowing gowns with no corset underneath. Fans bought the Castles' book *Modern Dancing* and read articles about them in *Ladies' Home Journal*.

Vernon joined the British army as a pilot in 1915. Irene stayed on Broadway until 1916, before starring in the silent movie *Patria*. Vernon died in a plane crash during the war. Irene retired from show business in the mid-1920s, remarried several times, and died in 1969.

" PARTED BY DANCE CRAZE; Wife Says Husband Left Her to Fox Trot with Young Women."

—*New York Times* headline, 1915

U.S. SOLDIERS ON LEAVE LISTEN TO A PIANO PERFORMANCE with their wives at a soldiers' social club in 1918.

As the nation mobilized for war, patriotic music began to drown out the opposition. John Philip Sousa, former conductor of the U.S. Marine Band, composed several new patriotic marches, including "America First" (1916), "The Naval Reserve" (1917), and "Anchor and Star" (1918). George M. Cohan's defiant "Over There" (1917) told Europe to get ready because the "Yanks" were coming to fight and would not quit until the job was done "over there."

Boys prepare for a CRATE SCOOTER RACE on the streets of New York City in 1910.

CHAPTER TEN

FUN AND GAMES:
SPORTS IN THE 1910s

W hen Americans of the 1910s weren't working, they wanted to have fun. Children played ball in empty city lots and alleys. Both adults and children rode bicycles. Those who could afford membership in a pricy country club played golf and tennis. Young men joined high school and college sports teams, although schools offered few sports for young women during this era. Cars offered recreation as well as transportation. Families packed into autos for a Sunday drive in the country or a vacation at a faraway park, forest, or resort. Meanwhile, manufacturers cashed in on the public's enthusiasm by launching a thriving sporting goods industry. They made products and clothes to suit every athletic pursuit.

■ FAN FAVORITES

Americans of the 1910s also loved to watch top athletes perform. Students and alumni cheered for their favorite college football teams (professional football was only loosely organized at this time). The game of football changed dramatically in the 1910s when teams began using a new offensive technique—the forward pass. Only recently sanctioned by college football officials, the pass enabled unheralded Notre Dame to defeat powerhouse Army (the U.S. Military Academy) in a dramatic upset in 1913. The Notre Dame quarterback in that game was Gus Dorais, and the pass receiver was Knute Rockne, who went on to greater fame as Notre Dame's coach.

121

Of all the star athletes of the 1910s, boxer Jack Johnson caused the greatest controversy. Johnson, an African American, was born in Galveston, Texas, in 1878. He dropped out of school after only five years and worked odd jobs to earn money. In his teens, he took up boxing. He had his first professional bout in 1897.

Johnson racked up a string of victories in the early 1900s, although many white boxers refused to fight him because he was black. In 1908 white heavyweight champion Tommy Burns agreed to fight Johnson. Johnson defeated Burns in fourteen rounds to become the heavyweight champion of the world.

Although Johnson became a hero to many African Americans, many boxing fans despised him—both for his race and for his marriages to white women. Interracial marriage was against the law in this era, but as one reporter remarked, Johnson "was completely fearless, [and] refused to kowtow to custom or law, disdaining social conventions."

Boxing promoters searched for a white man who could defeat Johnson—a "great white hope" who would take back the heavyweight title. In 1910 Jim Jeffries, a retired former champion, agreed to fight Johnson. But Jeffries was in poor shape and lost badly. After the fight, whites attacked African Americans in several U.S. cities. The Texas legislature even banned films that showed Johnson beating white opponents.

JACK JOHNSON smiles during a training session in the mid-1910s.

In 1913 federal agents convicted Johnson of violating the Mann Act, which prohibited the transportation of women across state lines for immoral purposes. Historians believe the government simply wanted to punish Johnson for his relationships with white women. Before the case was resolved, Johnson fled the United States, going first to Canada and then several other nations.

He continued to box in foreign countries. In 1915 he lost his title to Jess Willard in a match in Cuba. When he returned to the United States in 1920, he served ten months in jail for his 1913 conviction. After his release, Johnson continued to box. He retired from boxing in 1928. He then worked in several different businesses before dying in a car crash in 1946.

SIR BARTON *(back)* runs a warm-up lap with Man o' War *(front)* at a Canadian track in 1920. Americans of the 1910s loved betting on horse races.

Boxing was popular with sports fans in the 1910s, as was horse racing. In 1919 a horse named Sir Barton became racing's first Triple Crown winner (by winning the Kentucky Derby, Preakness Stakes, and Belmont Stakes all in one year).

Even though Americans were crazy for sports in the 1910s, they might not have known much about the Olympic Games in this decade. The modern games (based on contests in ancient Greece) were just getting organized after being revived in 1896. In 1912 a team of U.S. athletes, including track-and-field star Jim Thorpe, traveled to the games in Stockholm, Sweden. The U.S. athletes took home twenty-five gold medals from those games—more golds than any other nation. Most Americans learned about the victories by reading newspaper reports. They were proud of the U.S. athletes, but most were far more interested in the exploits of their favorite baseball and football teams. (The 1916 Olympic Games were canceled due to World War I.)

JIM THORPE jumps hurdles at an athletic meet for Olympic athletes in Reims, France, in 1912.

Multitalented Jim Thorpe was a standout in three different sports: football, track and field, and baseball. He played them all at the highest level in the 1910s. A Native American, Thorpe was born in 1887 in Oklahoma. As a boy, he attended several Indian schools. These schools forced Native American children to cast off their native customs and act more like white Americans.

Thorpe's last school was the Carlisle Indian Industrial School in Carlisle, Pennsylvania. It trained students at both the high school and college level. At Carlisle, Thorpe played football and baseball and ran track. In the early 1910s, Thorpe led the Carlisle football team to victories against the best college teams of the era.

In 1912 Thorpe earned a spot on the U.S. Olympic team and headed to the Olympic Games in Stockholm, Sweden. There he won two gold medals—in the pentathlon (a five-event track-and-field contest) and the decathlon (ten events). Shortly afterward, a reporter discovered that Thorpe had once earned money playing minor-league base-ball in summer. Officials ruled that Thorpe was therefore not an amateur athlete and should not have been allowed to compete in the amateur-only Olympics. The International Olympic Committee (IOC) took away Thorpe's gold medals.

After this disappointment, Thorpe moved on to a career in professional sports. He played baseball from 1913 to 1919 and played football from 1915 to 1928. In 1920 Thorpe helped organize the American Professional Football Association (the modern-day National Football League).

After Thorpe retired from football, he pursued a number of different interests. He acted in movies, fought for Native American rights, and organized the Junior Olympics for young athletes. In 1950 sports organizations began to recognize Thorpe for his achievements earlier in the century. But the greatest honors came long after Thorpe died in 1953. Most importantly, historians discovered that Thorpe's Olympic medals had been wrongly taken away in 1912. In 1982 the IOC restored his name to the record books and gave duplicates of his two gold medals to his children.

■ "TAKE ME OUT TO THE BALL GAME"

Baseball was by far the nation's favorite spectator sport in the 1910s—labeled the national pastime. Two professional leagues, the National and the American, held games in most major cities. Midsized towns hosted amateur teams. At stadiums throughout the nation, fans sang "Take Me Out to the Ball Game" (written in 1908) and cheered their favorite players.

Big-league stars included Detroit Tigers slugger Ty Cobb, Pittsburgh Pirates shortstop Honus Wagner, Chicago White Sox outfielder "Shoeless" Joe Jackson. All these players were white because baseball was strictly segregated in this era. The big leagues didn't allow black players. African

> **" Now the speed-crazed comet dashes up and down the third-base line. . . . Will Cobb have the nerve to try to steal home? You said it; he will."**
>
> —**New York Times** *report on Detroit Tiger Ty Cobb, 1915*

125

Detroit Tigers star **TY COBB** at bat during a 1913 game.

Americans played on all-black teams such as the Birmingham Black Barons and the Chicago American Giants (in the 1920s, the African American teams were organized into the Negro Leagues).

George "Babe" Ruth shot into the spotlight during the 1910s. Other players on his minor-league Baltimore Orioles team nicknamed him Babe because he was only nineteen when he joined the team in 1914. But his ace pitching and powerful hitting earned him the respect of more seasoned players. Later that year, Ruth joined the Boston Red Sox as a pitcher. His home run record, strong pitching arm, and lively personality made him one of the most popular players of the 1910s, but his real fame came in the 1920s when he joined the New York Yankees.

In the fall of 1919, scandal marred the national pastime. The Chicago White Sox were favored to win the World Series but instead suffered a surprising loss to the Cincinnati Reds. Shortly after the game, rumors leaked that eight Chicago players, including Shoeless Joe Jackson, had taken payoffs from professional gamblers to throw, or lose, the game. Even worse, they had bet against their own team. Fans reacted with disbelief. Legend states that a teary-eyed boy pleaded with Shoeless Joe Jackson, "Say it ain't so, Joe." Jackson responded, "Yes, kid, I'm afraid it is."

In the end, a Chicago grand jury cleared seven players and let the eighth go for lack of evidence. But the baseball commissioner permanently banned the eight players from professional baseball. After the "Black Sox" scandal, some reporters predicted that baseball would never bounce back. True fans, however, refused to stay away for long.

SHOELESS JOE JACKSON was involved in the "Black Sox" baseball scandal of 1919.

■ ON WHEELS

Bicycles, which had arrived in large numbers on U.S. roads in the late 1800s, remained popular in the 1910s. People bicycled mostly for recreation and sometimes for transportation.

Some Americans liked to race bicycles. Races took place in velodromes—steeply banked oval tracks with smooth wooden riding surfaces. Fans especially loved six-day competitions, during which racers circled velodromes or rode country paths for almost a week, with only short breaks for sleep and food.

One of the greatest bicycle racers of the era was Frank Kramer. He won sixteen straight U.S. cycling championships, from 1901 to 1916. By the late teens, his salary topped twenty thousand dollars a year, making him one of the highest-paid athletes of the decade.

The popularity of cycle racing waned as automobile races attracted a greater following. Fans preferred the higher speeds. Race-car driver Barney Oldfield was the speed king, setting automobile speed records throughout the first decade of the twentieth century. He shocked everyone in 1910, when he set a speed record of more than 131 miles (211 km) per hour on a racetrack in Daytona, Florida.

The Indianapolis 500 began in 1911. In this race, drivers maneuvered their cars around a track, the Indianapolis Motor Speedway, for 500 miles (804 km). The event quickly became the most popular car race in the United States.

BARNEY OLDFIELD pits his race car against an airplane in a 1914 race.

Singers and dancers put on a JAZZ AND BLUES REVUE at Chicago's Sunset Club in 1922.

EPILOGUE
THE MODERN WAY

The 1910s left a huge legacy for the next generation. The great events of the decade—World War I, woman suffrage, new technology, labor struggles, and the Prohibition amendment—brought sweeping changes to the United States in the 1920s.

On the positive side, new technology, such as cars, electric lights, and telephones, made life more convenient, comfortable, and efficient. New technology also speeded up business operations. The arts of the 1910s—everything from jazz music to moving pictures to the Armory Show—introduced Americans to new images, sounds, and ideas. These new sights and sounds would become even more pronounced in the following decade, which came to be called the Roaring Twenties.

Woman suffrage opened up a new world for U.S. women. With the right to vote, women of the 1920s could play a more active role in government and community. They went on to take part in political campaigns, run for office themselves and, in a few cases, take high positions in U.S. government. Women also became more daring in the 1920s, experimenting with everything from shorter skirts to smoking.

The big changes of the 1910s brought many negatives as well. The decade ended with continuing labor dissatisfaction, the Palmer Raids, and an anti-immigrant fervor.

The 1920s were marked by tight restrictions on immigration, bigotry against foreign-born Americans, and a squelching of labor unions. The racial hatred and violence of the 1910s continued in the 1920s, especially with the resurgence of the Ku Klux Klan.

The Prohibition amendment did not turn out the way prohibitionists had planned when they fought for it in the 1910s. Specifically, Prohibition did not wipe out crime, vice, and poverty. Instead, once it became illegal to manufacture and sell alcohol, scores of underground enterprises sprang up. Gangsters and smugglers sold liquor illegally and bribed law enforcement officers to look the other way. People bought booze on the sly and sometimes got sick from drinking homemade liquor. In many cases, the dealings turned deadly, as rival gangs battled one another for control of the illegal liquor trade. Eventually Americans agreed that Prohibition had been a failure, and in 1933, the states repealed the amendment.

Finally, World War I took a great toll on the nation. After the war, citizens celebrated a much-welcomed peace. But war had traumatized the United States. Thousands of U.S. soldiers had been killed or wounded. The economy had boomed briefly but then

Patrons of a **NEW YORK CITY SPEAKEASY** enjoy jazz music and illegal liquor in the early 1920s.

AMERICA THE 1910s

THE 369TH INFANTRY REGIMENT RETURNS HOME TO NEW YORK at the end of World War I. These and many other African American soldiers fought bravely and received awards for their service in Europe. They returned to find that racial prejudice still barred their way to success.

sank down after the war, and many returning soldiers couldn't find jobs. Many Americans felt that interfering in Europe's fight hadn't been worth the cost. They thought the United States should retreat from international politics, which is just what happened in the 1920s.

On November 2, 1920, fifty-five-year-old Warren Harding was elected the twenty-ninth U.S. president. By then Americans were tired of radical politics, tired of war, and tired of worrying about the rest of the world. Harding pledged to help the nation get on a normal footing again. "America's present need is not heroics," Harding said, "but restoration . . . not agitation, but adjustment . . . not the dramatic, but the dispassionate . . . not submergence in international-ity, but sustainment in triumphant nationality." Harding believed Americans needed to look inward to their own nation, and in the coming decade, that's exactly what they did.

1910
- Congress creates the postal savings bank system.
- William Boyce founds the Boy Scouts of America.
- Luther and Charlotte Gulick found the Camp Fire Girls.
- The NAACP magazine *Crisis*, edited by W. E. B. Du Bois, begins publication.
- The hobble skirt arrives in the United States from Paris.

1911
- Charles Kettering invents the electric self-starting motor for cars.
- The Triangle Shirtwaist Factory fire kills 146 textile workers in New York City.
- *Ethan Frome*, by Edith Wharton, is published.
- Irving Berlin writes "Alexander's Ragtime Band."
- The Indianapolis 500 auto race begins in Indianapolis.

1912
- Theodore Roosevelt runs for president on the Progressive Party ticket.
- The luxury ship *Titanic* hits an iceberg and sinks in the North Atlantic Ocean.
- Woodrow Wilson becomes the twenty-eighth president of the United States.
- Lester Wire devises the first electric traffic light.
- Jim Thorpe competes in the 1912 Olympics in Stockholm, Sweden.

1913
- The Sixteenth Amendment establishes a federal income tax.
- Congress passes the Federal Reserve Act, creating Federal Reserve Banks.
- Demonstrators march for woman suffrage before Woodrow Wilson's inauguration.
- The Armory Show introduces Americans to modern art.
- The first modern crossword puzzle appears in the *New York World*.
- The Notre Dame football team defeats Army by using the forward pass.

1914
- World War I (called the Great War in the 1910s) begins in Europe.
- The Ludlow massacre of striking coal miners occurs in Colorado.
- Mother's Day becomes a national holiday.
- Edgar Rice Burroughs publishes *Tarzan of the Apes*.

1915

- D. W. Griffith releases his controversial film *Birth of a Nation*.
- The Bell Telephone Company begins offering long-distance phone service.
- T. L. Williams founds the Maybelline company to sell mascara.
- *The Tramp*, starring Charlie Chaplin, plays in movie theaters.
- A firing squad executes labor leader Joe Hill.

1916

- Woodrow Wilson is elected to his second term as president.
- Jeanette Rankin becomes the first woman in the House of Representatives.
- John Dewey's *Democracy and Education* opens a new era in classroom teaching.
- John Lloyd Wright, son of architect Frank Lloyd Wright, creates Lincoln Logs.

1917

- The United States enters World War I.
- Congress passes the Espionage Act.
- The 1917 Immigration Act tightens restrictions on foreigners entering the United States.
- Protesters demonstrate for woman suffrage at the White House.
- George M. Cohan writes "Over There."

1918

- Congress passes the Sedition Act.
- World War I ends on November 11 at eleven in the morning.
- President Wilson introduces his Fourteen Points for postwar peace, including his idea for a League of Nations peacekeeping body.
- A worldwide flu epidemic begins.
- Willa Cather publishes *My Antonia*.

1919

- Attorney General Mitchell Palmer orders raids on labor and political organizations.
- Americans celebrate Armistice Day (later Veteran's Day) for the first time.
- The Nineteenth Amendment, giving women the right to vote, goes to the states for ratification.
- Congress passes the Volstead Act, which sets out the rules for Prohibition.
- Mary Pickford, Douglas Fairbanks, and Charlie Chaplin found the United Artists film studio.
- Eight Chicago White Sox players are accused of throwing the World Series and are banned from baseball.

SOURCE NOTES

5 Theodore Roosevelt Quotes, *iCelebZ.com*, 2006–2007, http://www.icelebz.com/quotes/theodore_roosevelt (February 4, 2009).

10 George Tindall, *America: A Narrative History* (New York: W. W. Norton and Company, 1992), 953.

14 *New York Times*, "Taft Bids Nation Be World Power," December 4, 1912, 6.

16 John Cooper Jr., *Pivotal Decades: The United States, 1900–1920* (New York: W. W. Norton, 1990), 155.

16 Walter Lord, *The Good Years: From 1900 to the First World War* (New York: Harper and Brothers, 1960), 317.

17 Harold Evans, *The American Century* (New York: Alfred A. Knopf, 2000),129.

18 Cooper, *Pivotal Decades*, 181.

19 Eugene Debs, "Speech of Acceptance," *International Socialist Review* (October 1912). Available online at *History Matters*, "Debs Attacks 'the Monstrous System' of Capitalism," n.d., http://historymatters.gmu.edu/d/5725 (June 7, 2009).

19 Evans, *American Century*, 129

21 Philip B. Kunhardt Jr., *The American President* (New York: Penguin, 1999), 325.

21 Arthur Schlesinger Jr. ed., *The Almanac of American History* (New York: Barnes and Noble Books, 1993), 423.

23 Schlesinger, *Almanac of American History*, 326.

24 Ibid., 426.

26 Lorraine Glennon, ed., *Our Times: The Illustrated History of the Twentieth Century* (Atlanta: Turner Publishing, 1995), 115.

26 *New York Times*, "Same Till End of Time," May 12, 1915, 4.

28 Cooper, *Pivotal Decades*, 248.

29 Kunhardt, *American President*, 326.

30 Ibid.

31 Adrienne Drell, ed., *Twentieth Century Chicago: 100 Years, 100 Voices* (Chicago: Sports Publishing, 2000), 49.

33 Ronald Schaffer, *America in the Great War: The Rise of the War Welfare State* (New York: Oxford University Press, 1991), 15.

36 Drell, *Twentieth-Century Chicago*, 48–49.

37 Gordon Edlin and Eric Golanty, *Health and Wellness* (Boston: Jones and Bartlett, 2006), 264.

38 Evans, *American Century*, 167.

39 Samuel Morison, *A Concise History of the American Republic* (New York: Oxford University Press, 1977), 560.

43 Jim Murphy, "Hundred Years of Wheels and Wings," in James Cross Giblin, ed., *The Century That Was: Reflections on the Last Hundred Years* (New York: Atheneum, 2000), 64.

47 Early Radio History, "Pre-War Vacuum-Tube Transmitter Development (1914–1917)," n.d., *United States Early Radio History*, 2009, http://earlyradiohistory.us/1916rmb.htm (June 7, 2009).

53 Glennon, *Our Times*, 83.

56 Eleanor Flexner, *Century of Struggle: The Women's Movement in the United States*. (Cambridge, MA: Belknap Press, 1975), 248.

57 Glenda Riley, *Inventing the American Woman: A Perspective on Women's History 1865 to the Present* (Arlington Heights, IL: Harlan Davidson, 1986), 5.

60 Anarchy for Anybody, "The Ludlow Massacre," *Capital Offenses*, n.d. http://a4a.mahost.org/ludlow.html (June 7, 2009).

61 Ibid.

62 *New York Times*, "Says Only Wilson Can Settle Strike," May 20, 1914, 5.

62 *New York Times*, "Colorado Senate Condemns Ammons," May 8, 1914, 6.

71 Anne Rice, *Witnessing Lynching: American Writers Respond* (New York: Rutgers University Press, 2003), 174.

73 Julie Roy Jeffrey, *The American People: Creating a Nation and Society* (New York: HarperCollins, 1990), 727.

74 Evans, *American Century*, 192.

75 T. Minihan, "The Teacher Goes Job-Hunting," *Nation* 124 (1927) 606.

76 Lord, *Good Years*, 283.

78 United States Senate, "September 30, 1918, a Vote for Women," *United States Senate*, 2009, http://senate.gov/artandhistory/

history/minute/A_Vote_For_Women.htm (June 7, 2009).

79 Evans, *American Century*, 123.

81 P. H. Odegard, *Pressure Politics: The Story of the Anti Saloon League* (New York: Columbia University Press, 1928), 72.

81 Library of Congress, "Today in History: October 28," *Library of Congress*, 2009, http://memory.loc.gov/ammem/today/oct28.html (June 7, 2009).

83 Dewey, John, *Democracy and Education* (New York: Macmillan, 1916), 228.

84 Camp Fire USA, "All About Us—History," *Camp Fire USA*, 2009, http://www.campfireusa.org/all_about_us/history.asp (June 7, 2009).

88 *New York Times*, "Notable Books in Brief Reviews," June 11, 1916, BR242.

91 Evans, *American Century*, 151.

91 National Geographic editors, *Eyewitness to the Twentieth Century* (Washington, DC: National Geographic Society, 1998), 77.

95 Frank L. Wright, *The Natural House* (New York: Horizon Press, 1954), 16.

97 Ibid., 122.

100 AdClassix, "1919 H&W Brassieres," *AdClassix.com*, 2009, http://www.adclassix.com/ads/19hwbrassieres.htm (June 7, 2009).

101 Jack Cassin-Scott, *Costume and Fashion in Color 1760–1920* (New York: Macmillan, 1971), 201.

107 Glennon, *Our Times*, 115.

109 Ibid., 104.

115 Ibid., 108.

118 *New York Times*, "Parted by Dance Craze; Wife Says Husband Left Her to Fox Trot with Young Women, January 7, 1915, 22.

122 Al-Tony Gilmore, "Jack Johnson: A Magnificent Black Anachronism of the Early Twentieth Century," *Journal of Social and Behavioral Sciences* 19 (Winter 1973): 35–42.

125 *New York Times*, "Ty Cobb's Daring Upsets Yankees," June 15, 1915, 10.

126 Arthur Daly, "The Sports of the Times: Say It Ain't So, Joe." *New York Times*, January 18, 1951.

131 White House, "Warren G. Harding," *The White House*, 2009, http://whitehouse.gov/about/presidents/WarrenHarding (June 7, 2009).

SELECTED BIBLIOGRAPHY

Caplow, Theodore, Louis Hicks, and Ben Wattenberg. *The First Measured Century: An Illustrated Guide to Trends in America, 1900–2000*. Washington, DC: AEI Press, 2001.
This fascinating book offers statistics on life in the twentieth century, including trends in business, politics, work, education, family life, religion, and money.

Cassin-Scott, Jack. *Costume and Fashion in Color, 1760–1920*. New York: Macmillan Company, 1971.
This illustrated title chronicles fashions for men and women over a span of 160 years.

Cooper, John, Jr. *Pivotal Decades: The United States, 1900–1920*. New York: W. W. Norton, 1990.
The early 1900s were critical years in U.S. politics. The author examines these years in great detail.

Evans, Harold. *The American Century*. New York: Alfred A. Knopf, 2000.
Evans offers fascinating insights into various aspects of the 1910s and other decades of the twentieth century.

Ewing, Elizabeth. *History of Twentieth-Century Fashion*. Lanham, MD: Barnes and Noble Books, 1989.
This book focuses on twentieth-century clothing styles, including fashions of the 1910s.

Flexner. Eleanor. *Century of Struggle: The Woman's Rights Movement in the United States*. Cambridge, MA: Belknap Press, 1975.
Flexnor's book is one of the most complete histories of the U.S. women's rights movement, with extensive coverage of the movement for woman suffrage.

Gardner, Louise, *Art through the Ages*. New York: Harcourt, Brace and World, 1959.
A classic in art history, this title examines art trends over time, including modern art movements of the early twentieth century.

Grunwald, Lisa. *Women's Letters: America from the Revolutionary War to the Present*. New York: Dial Press, 2001.
This book brings U.S. history to life by reprinting the letters of ordinary women, such as those who fought for woman suffrage in the early 1900s.

Jennings, Peter. *The Century*. New York: Doubleday, 2001.
Written by one of the nation's most celebrated investigative reporters, this review of the twentieth century includes a variety of fascinating facts.

Lord, Walter. *The Good Years: From 1900 to the First World War*. New York: Harper and Brothers, 1960.
Lord explores the 1900s and 1910s, how the two decades compared and differed, and the events leading up to World War I.

Morris, Edmund. *Theodore Rex*. New York: Random House, 2001.
This insightful biography takes a thorough look at the life of President Theodore Roosevelt.

Schlesinger, Arthur, Jr., ed. *The Almanac of American History*. New York: Barnes and Noble Books, 1993.
This detailed review of U.S. history chronicles the people and events that molded the nation.

Time-Life editors. *People Who Shaped the Century*. Alexandria, VA: Time-Life Books, 1999.
This title, organized by decade, highlights individuals who made a great imprint on twentieth-century history.

TO LEARN MORE

Books

Bartoletti, Susan Campbell. *Kids on Strike!* Boston: Houghton Mifflin, 1999.
Many labor activists in the early twentieth century were child workers. This fascinating title tells the stories of these young laborers.

Benson, Michael. *William Howard Taft*. Minneapolis: Twenty-First Century Books, 2005.
The biography covers Taft's life and work, including his supervision of the Panama Canal project and his term as president of the United States.

Brill, Marlene Targ. *Women for Peace*. New York: Franklin Watts, 1997.
This book tells how women have played a key role in peace movements from ancient to modern times. It includes information on women who fought for peace while the rest of the world was gearing up for World War I.

Callan, Jim. *America in the 1900s and 1910s*. New York: Facts on File, 2006.
The title paints a detailed and engaging portrait of U.S. life in the early twentieth century.

Feinstein, Stephen. *The 1910s*. Berkeley Heights, NJ: Enslow Publishers, 2001.
In this richly illustrated title, the author presents social, cultural, and historic highlights of the 1910s.

Feldman, Ruth Tenzer. *World War I*. Minneapolis: Twenty-First Century Books, 2004.
This comprehensive book for young readers details World War I from many angles, with coverage of the battles, the soldiers, the weapons, the politicians, and life on the home front.

Giblin, James Cross, ed. *That Century That Was: Reflections on the Last One Hundred Years*. New York: Atheneum Books, 2000.
This book highlights key events in U.S. history by topic, with each chapter written by a different well-known author of children's nonfiction.

Golus, Carrie. *Jim Thorpe*. Minneapolis: Twenty-First Century Books, 2008.
This fascinating biography traces the life of superathlete Jim Thorpe. A Native American, Thorpe endured many setbacks, from racial discrimination to the loss of his Olympic medals. But he also experienced many triumphs.

Gourley, Catherine. *Gibson Girls and Suffragists: Perceptions of Women from 1900 to 1918*. Minneapolis: Twenty-First Century Books, 2008.
This appealing selection examines advertising, film, and other media to explore views on American women in the early twentieth century.

McPherson, Stephanie. *Theodore Roosevelt*. Minneapolis: Twenty-First Century Books, 2005.
This book provides interesting information about Theodore Roosevelt, the twenty-sixth president of the United States.

Mee, Sue. *1900–20: Linen and Lace*. Milwaukee: Gareth Stevens, 2000.
The author discusses two decades of women's fashion, explaining how clothing styles reflected trends in U.S. society.

Wels, Susan. *Titanic: Legacy of the World's Greatest Ocean Liner*. New York: Time-Life Books, 1997.
The book describes the excitement around *Titanic*'s maiden voyage and the tragedy of its sinking.

Skurzynski, Gloria. *Sweat and Blood: A History of U.S. Labor Unions*. Minneapolis: Twenty-First Century Books, 2009.
The history of how brave working people struggled to gain fair wages, reasonable hours, and secure lives by forming labor unions.

Films

Influenza 1918, DVD. Arlington, VA: PBS, 2006.
Part of the acclaimed *American Experience* series, this documentary examines the worldwide flu epidemic of 1918–1919—which proved far more deadly than World War I.

One Woman, One Vote, DVD. Arlington, VA: PBS, 2006.
The struggle for woman suffrage was long and arduous, but it finally paid off with the passage of the Nineteenth Amendment. This documentary traces the movement from start to finish.

Woodrow Wilson, DVD. New York: A&E Home Video, 2006.
As president, Woodrow Wilson struggled with a profound question—whether the United States should enter World War I. This in-depth biography traces Wilson's rise from scholar to politician to wartime president.

Websites

America's Story from America's Library
http://www.americaslibrary.gov
This site from the Library of Congress includes biographies of famous Americans, original historic documents, and discussions about different periods in U.S. history.

The Great War and the Shaping of the Twentieth Century
http://www.pbs.org/greatwar/
A companion to the PBS television series, this website offers extensive coverage of World War I, including maps, quotes, audio clips, and a timeline.

Unforgivable Blackness: The Rise and Fall of Jack Johnson
http://www.pbs.org/unforgivableblackness/
This website is a companion to the award-winning Ken Burns film of the same name. The site examines Johnson's boxing career in the context of attitudes about race and sex in the early twentieth century.

SELECTED 1910s CLASSICS

Books

Burroughs, Edgar Rice. *Tarzan of the Apes*. 1914. Reprint, New York: Signet Classics, 2008.
This classic tales introduces Tarzan, the son of a British nobleman who is abandoned in the African jungle and raised by a family of apes. Tarzan grows up to be a brave jungle adventurer. After this book, Burroughs wrote twenty-five more books about Tarzan.

Cather, Willa. *My Antonia*. 1918. Reprint, New York: Signet Classics, 2005.
This classic from Willa Cather tells the story of Antonia Shimerda, a Bohemian immigrant to Nebraska. Told through the eyes of her neighbor Jim Burden, the novel shows Antonia's determination to survive on the untamed prairie.

Johnson, James Weldon. *The Autobiography of an Ex-Coloured Man*. 1912. Reprint, New York: Hill and Wang, 1991.
This fictional memoir tells the story of a light-skinned African American man who is able to pass for white. The book paints a vivid picture of racial attitudes at the turn of the twentieth century.

Films

A Fool There Was. New York: Kino Video, 2002.
Dark-eyed Theda Bara shocked straight-laced Americans when she played the vamp on-screen. In this silent film from 1915, she utters the classic line, "Kiss me, my fool."

The Little Tramp: The Charlie Chaplin Collection. North Hollywood, CA: Passport Video, 2006.
This five-disc collection contains more than forty short Chaplin films from the years 1914 to 1922. Movies such as *The Tramp* and *The Floorwalker* show Chaplin at his best.

Mary Pickford Signature Collection. Woodland Hills, CA: St. Clair Entertainment, 2008.
In the days of silent film, wholesome Mary Pickford was called America's Sweetheart. This DVD collection contains four of her best-loved films, *Poor Little Rich Girl*, *Rebecca of Sunnybrook Farm*, *Pollyanna*, and *Little Annie Rooney*.

Identify six to ten things in everyday life that relate to the early 1910s. (To get started, consider family antiques or collections, your house or buildings in your neighborhood, movies, books, or songs you may have heard of, and places you've visited.) Use photographs, mementos, and words to create a paper or electronic scrapbook of your 1910s connections.

INDEX

142

143

ABOUT THE AUTHOR

Marlee Richards is an award-winning author of many books for readers of all ages. Her passion is writing about key events in history and the people who made them possible. Richards lives with her husband near Chicago, Illinois.

PHOTO ACKNOWLEDGMENTS

The images in this book are used with the permission of: US National Archives/ War and Conflict Collection, pp. 3, 30, 36, 56, 64, 91,119, 131, 141 (bottom left); © Ann Ronan Picture Library/HIP/The Image Works, pp. 4–5; © Roger Viollet/The Image Works, pp. 7 (top),124; © Sueddeutsche Zeltung Photo/The Image Works, p. 8; Library of Congress: (LC–USZ62–59520), p. 9; (LC–USZ62–67666), p. 10; (LC_DIG_hec–03152), pp. 12–13; (LC–DIG–hec–03137), p. 14; (LC–USZ62–96924), p. 15; (LC–USZC4–10297), p. 29; (LC–USZ62–11417), p. 32; (LC–DIG-hec-03825), p. 34; (LC–USZ62–107409), p. 45; (LC–USZ62–116256), p. 46; (LC–USZ62–7678), p. 60; (LC–USZ62–38100), p. 62; (LC–DIG-ggbain-22834), p. 69; (LC–USZ62–114302), p. 71; (LC–USZ62–16767), p. 72; (LC–USZ62–22262), pp. 76–77; (LC–USZ62–37937), p. 78; (LC–USZ62–29808), p. 79; (LC–USZ62–109744), p. 84; (LC–USZ62–29408), p. 88; (LC–USZ62–82914), p. 89; (LC–USZC4–13057), p. 90; (LC–USZ62–127226), p. 95; (LC_DIG–ncLC–01284), p. 102; (LC–USZ62–64085), p. 114; (LC–USZ62–120466), p. 118; (LC–USZ6–1826), p. 122; (LC–DIG–hec-02753), p. 125; (LC–DIG–ggbain-25393), p. 126; (LC–USZ62–22262), p. 141 (top); (LC–USZ62–120466), p. 141 (right); © Topham/The Image Works, pp. 16, 35; The Art Archive/Culver Pictures, p. 17; © TopFoto/The Image Works, pp. 18, 27, 38; CSU Archives/Everett Collection, p. 20; © Bettmann/CORBIS, pp. 21, 25, 28, 80, 92–93,123; The Granger Collection, New York, pp. 22–23, 37, 75, 82, 86–87, 96,130; © Mary Evans Picture Library/The Image Works, pp. 24, 48, 51, 81, 98, 99; © Photo12/The Image Works, pp. 31, 33; © akg-images/The Image Works, pp. 40–41,115; © Boyer/Roger-Viollet/The Image Works, p. 42; Wisconsin Historical Society/Everett Collection, pp. 43, 97, 112–113; © Maurice Branger/Roger-Viollet/The Image Works, p. 44; © White Packert/Getty Images, p. 47; © Underwood and Underwood/CORBIS, p. 49;Courtesy of the National Library of Medicine, p. 50; © Todd Strand/Independent Picture Service, p. 52; ©Alinari Archives/The Image Works, p. 53; ©National Media Museum/SSPL/The Image Works, pp. 54–55; Everett Collection, pp. 57,101,103,106, 108, 111; © Sueddeutsche Zeitung Photo/The Image Works, p. 58; Sharlot Hall Museum Archives Prescott, AZ, pp. 59, 65; The Denver Public Library, Western History Collection, (Z-193), p. 61; Henry A. Briol/Minnesota Historical Society, pp. 66–67; © J.J Lambe/Hulton Archive/Getty Images, p. 68; © Hulton Archive/Getty Images, pp. 70, 73 (bottom), 104–5; © The Museum of Modern Art/Licensed by Scala/Art Resource, NY, used with permission of Joanna T. Steichen, p. 94; © US National Archives/Roger-Viollet/The Image Works, p. 100; © Schenectady Museum/Hall of Electricity Foundation/CORBIS, p. 107; Keysone Film Company/The Kobal Collection, p. 109; © American Stock./Hulton Archive/Getty Images, p. 110; The New York Public Library for the Performing Arts/Music Division, Astor, Lenox and Tilden Foundations or Picture Collection, The Branch Libraries, The New York Public Library, Astor, Lenox and Tilden Foundations, pp. 116, 117 (right); © Albert Harlingue/Roger-Viollet/The Image Works, p. 117 (left); © Lewis W. Hine/Hulton Archive/Getty Images, p. 120–121; © Topical Press Agency/Hulton Archive/Getty Images, p. 127; © Frank Driggs Collection/Hulton Archive/Getty Images, pp. 128–9.

Front cover: © Mary Evans Picture Library /The Image Works (top left); © Underwood & Underwood/CORBIS (top right); © MPI/Getty Images (bottom left); © Hulton Archive/Getty Images (bottom right).